CRITICAL APPROACHES
TO MEDIEVAL LITERATURE

CRITICAL APPROACHES TO MEDIEVAL LITERATURE

SELECTED PAPERS FROM THE ENGLISH INSTITUTE, 1958–1959

EDITED WITH A FOREWORD BY DOROTHY BETHURUM

COLUMBIA UNIVERSITY PRESS: NEW YORK AND LONDON

First printing 1960
Fourth printing 1967

Library of Congress Catalog Card Number: 60–13104
Printed in the United States of America

FOREWORD

WE ARE NOW in what medievalists are about to convince themselves is a real renaissance of interest in the literature of the Middle Ages. Perhaps it began with the poets, for Eliot and Pound and Yeats all sent the scholars scurrying to Arthurian romances with their Celtic echoes and to Old French, Provençal, and early Italian metrical forms; but it has by now aroused in the scholars a concern with medieval literature for its own sake. The poets' medievalism may still be that of the early Romantics; the growing interest of critics both arises from and issues in a wide variety of approaches to medieval literature, the application of various disciplines to its study. The attitude of two generations ago is still reflected in the division of the English School in British universities: the study of all literature before Chaucer is classified as language, that of subsequent works as literature. But in both England and America the revolt against philology has gone far, perhaps too far; and now the employment of many ancillary disciplines in the study of early literature is made, one sometimes fears, at the expense of a sound knowledge of Old and Middle English as languages.

The method that has aroused the most disputatious comment recently is that treated in the first three papers of this volume, the application of patristic exegesis to the study of medieval literature. It arose, doubtless, from an attempt to fill out the intellectual background of various authors by discovering and recalling to a secular age commonly accepted religious beliefs as defined by orthodox authority. Since the method of the Fathers in explicating scriptural texts is usually what we loosely call allegorical, the expounding of nonliteral meanings, those who apply this exegesis to literature have become known in current critical jargon as the "allegorists." It is not a wholly exact term, though much of their work does aim at establishing symbolic, typological, or allegorical meanings. Controversy has flourished on the meaning of the central symbol in *Pearl,* for example, and on the deviations from a literal reading of the text necessary to elicit the poem's riches. Similarly with *Piers Plowman,* some of Chaucer's work, the Arthurian romances, and secular lyrics; it is often claimed that the kernel can be uncovered only by the exegetical method.

A somewhat less exact application of the allegorical method has been made to such secular works as *Troilus and Criseyde,* the *Roman de la Rose,* or Chrétien's *Percival* on the assumption that a major writer of the Middle Ages must set forth somehow the Christian scheme of redemption with its concomitant view of charity as the supreme virtue. Here very often the critic attempts a reconciliation of the doctrines of secular love—courtly love, as the term is commonly used—and the teachings of the Church about charity. Other assumptions underlying this work are that orthodox belief did not change from Origen to Thomas Aquinas and that patristic pronouncements, even obscure ones, were available to most writers, or, if not that, then that these ideas and beliefs were widely current and formed the intellectual stock-in-trade of medieval writers through the fourteenth century.

Objections have been raised to this method and to these assumptions from several quarters. Probably the basic one concerns whether there was in the Middle Ages any literature written outside the aura of religious preoccupation. This issue becomes acute in the case of the Arthurian romances particularly, in Chaucer's work, and in the apparently secular lyrics which have been read as religious in meaning. The use of sexual imagery in religious writings by the twelfth-century mystics, St. Bernard for example, further complicates the problem and has led to a reinterpretation of troubadour songs as religious in meaning and not amorous, which, in turn, has been vigorously questioned by opponents of this method.

More often opposition comes on specific interpretations of passages where skeptical critics feel the sense is forced, or the language not properly understood, or the total meaning of a poem such as *Troilus and Criseyde* warped by the application of patristic exegesis. Sometimes the question is disputed whether the fourfold interpretation of scripture practiced by the Fathers is applicable to anything but Holy Writ, and this is particularly pertinent in the writings on the *Pearl*. Here, too, Dante's famous letter to Can Grande has come in for a good deal of comment.

With all this ferment present the English Institute thought it wise to plan a debate on the subject, hoping to distill from it good critical wine. E. Talbot Donaldson presented the case against the method and based it on what he considers specific misuses and misinterpretations of literature. Robert Kaske presented the case for it and likewise gave specific readings which he regards as an enrichment, if not the only possible meaning, of the passages in question. Finally, Charles Donahue summed up the debate by making a basic distinction between Hebrew typology and Hellenic allegory and by showing how and for what purpose the two were used by the Fathers from Origen to the thirteenth century.

The second medieval session of the Institute was less narrowly focused and explored several fields which have been profitably used in the criticism of pre-Tudor literature. Francis Utley has dealt with the most elusive and troublesome subjects—folklore, myth, and ritual. All have an uncommon tendency to shape-shifting, and it is very hard to establish the science of their metamorphoses. And not only do the elements in these fields constantly change within the discipline, but they violently cancel out each other. Is the bleeding lance in the *Perlesvaus,* for example, the Celtic Fairy Spear or the λόγχη of the Byzantine Mass? Is Gawain Cuchulain or John the Baptist? Clearly we have to do here with elements that need taming and stern disciplining to be widely useful, and they must be applied with common sense.

Richard Green discusses the use made of classical fable by the poets of the fourteenth century and illustrates it with passages from Chaucer. He is concerned with the iconographical significance of the fables and cites medieval encyclopedias and treatises where this science is set forth. Finally, Howard Schless takes up the now somewhat discredited study of sources and brings it to life again. Concentrating on Chaucer's indebtedness to Dante, he examines several passages Lowes attributed to Dante's influence and widens the range of investigation to illustrate what must be taken account of in the study of sources.

These papers by no means exhaust the methods by which medieval literature is being reappraised, but they do give evidence of its present vitality. They are not independent essays but make up a symposium, in which it is hoped that the reader will now take part.

Waterford, Connecticut DOROTHY BETHURUM
April, 1960

CONTENTS

PATRISTIC EXEGESIS IN THE CRITICISM OF MEDIEVAL LITERATURE

THE OPPOSITION

E. Talbot Donaldson

I AM NOT AWARE of any valid theoretical objection to the use of patristic exegesis in the criticism of medieval literature: if, as D. W. Robertson, Jr., says,[1] it is true that all serious poetry written by Christians during the Middle Ages promotes the doctrine of charity by using the same allegorical structure that the Fathers found in the Bible, then it follows that patristic exegesis alone will reveal the meaning of medieval poetry, and it would be sheer folly to disapprove of the fact. And even if one disbelieves, as I do, that the generality of good medieval poetry is such single-minded allegory, it would still be foolish to ignore the influence of the patristic tradition on medieval poetry, including that of the great poets Chaucer and Langland. But to admit such influence is not at all the same thing as admitting either that poetry which is nonallegorical in manner must be allegorical in meaning or that allegorical poetry which does not seem to be promoting charity must in fact be promoting it. There may be a handful of such poems, but I doubt that they are very good, or, if they are good, that they are good because they are cryptically allegorical or charity-promoting. In any case, I know of no such poems in Middle English, which is the only field in which I am competent. The patristic influence on Middle English poetry seems to me to consist in providing occasional symbols which by their rich tradition enhance the poetic contexts they appear in, but which are called into use naturally by those contexts and are given fresh meaning by them.

It is scarcely necessary to reassert the right of a poem to say what it means and mean what it says, and not what any one, before or after its composition, thinks it ought to say or mean. The existence of this right gives me, I hope, the right to test the validity of a kind of criticism which, it seems to me, imposes a categorical imperative upon the critic to operate in a certain way regardless of how the poem is telling him to operate. Since I lack a theoretical objection to patristic criticism as such, I can justify my opposition to it only by the invidious method of analyzing specific patristic critiques; but surely the burden of the proof is on the proponents of the critical method, who deny that I can understand what I read without possessing their special knowledge. To excuse my invidiousness I shall invoke a passage from the Scriptures: By their works ye shall know them. This I shall apply with twofold reference—though not, I trust, allegorically: that is, I shall apply it not only to those who try to prove the necessity for patristic exegesis, but also to the works in which this necessity is supposed to exist. I shall try to suggest that to give a reader a flat injunction to find one predetermined specific meaning in Middle English poetry is anything but the ideal way of preparing him to understand something old and difficult and complicated; for in his eagerness to find what must be there he will very likely miss what is there; and in so doing he may miss a meaning arising from the poem that is better than anything that exegesis is able to impose upon it. I hope I shall not offend any one if I suggest that while charity is the most important of doctrines it is not the only subject worth writing about, and that many poems may conduce to charity without mentioning it either specifically or allegorically. I may say rather ruefully that one of the natural disadvantages of the opponent of patristic criticism is that he is constantly being put in the position of seeming to deny that the Fall of Man has any dominant importance in the history of man's thought just because he denies that it has any relevance in a specific literary work. There are, indeed, moments when I could wish that scholars in Middle English literature would remind themselves that they are not angels but anglicists.

Having gone so far, I might go on to suggest that the Fathers of the Church were less expert at devising rules for poets than they were at devising rules for Christians. I am not, however, entirely persuaded that they did devise rules for poets. The case for the generalization that medieval poets were enjoined by patristic authority to write nothing but allegories supporting charity seems rather less than crystal-clear. It was natural that the fourfold method of scriptural interpretation should exert an influence on secular poets, especially in view of its occasional extension to the great pagan poets; and of course some medieval poets were, like Dante, deeply interested in exalting Christian doctrine through their poetry and consciously used allegory—even, perhaps, four-level allegory—to do so. But this does not mean that they all felt obliged to behave like Dante. I may quite well be wrong, but I cannot find that any of the patristic authorities ever clearly exhorted secular poets to write as the Bible had been written, even though the inference is pretty strong that some of them would have so exhorted if they had got round to it. But it seems to me that in order to find a definite injunction the modern critic has consciously to make a large inference.[2] Nor do I think that the case is much supported by the fact that in medieval schools reading was taught with attention to three matters, the *littera* or text, the *sensus* or narrative statement, and the *sententia* or theme, since the identification of *sententia* with an allegory promoting charity is itself no more than an inference.[3] After all, competent poetry has always contained something more than words making a statement, something that might well be called *sententia,* and I should imagine that Greeks, Romans, Arabs, Jews, and other non-Christians might inevitably teach poetry according to the same system: does the *Iliad* have no *sententia* because it is not Christian? Finally, there is at least one dissenting vote in the roll call of theologians presumably enjoining poets to write allegory after the example of Scripture. As W. K. Wimsatt pointed out in a paper on this topic several years ago,[4] Thomas Aquinas makes the unequivocal statement that "in no intellectual activity of the human mind can there properly speaking be found anything but literal sense: only in Scripture, of which the Holy Ghost was the author, man the instrument, can there be found" the spiritual sense—that is, the four levels of allegory.[5] While I recognize that St. Thomas is not a Father and that his statement may be idiosyncratic (as I believe some scholars regard it),[6] nevertheless I think he ought to be honestly reckoned with. To date I have seen no real discussion of his opinion by supporters of patristic exegesis. Nor will I accept as reputable the excuse that because he was a friar St. Thomas would hardly reflect the point of view of such medieval poets as favored the monks.[7]

I shall support my opposition to patristic exegesis in its extreme and most common form by examining three examples from its literature: critiques of *Piers Plowman,* of a poem by Chaucer, and of a Middle English lyric. I have naturally chosen the examples that seem to serve my purposes best, but this partiality is somewhat compensated for by the fact that these analyses have been taken as models by those who practice patristic exegesis. To the reasonable question of whether there are in existence specimens of patristic exegesis which do not arouse my opposition, I give a qualified yes; these concern poems where the Christian preoccupation is clearly a marked feature of the poem and where this sort of exegesis may help to enrich our appreciation of the poet's handiwork. My opposition begins, however, when the author of the critique tries to substitute a special meaning for the one the poem yields without exegesis, an attempt that is common enough to seem characteristic of the current school of exegetes.[8]

Christian preoccupation is certainly a marked feature of *Piers Plowman,* and on the surface of it the poem appears admirably suited to patristic exegesis. It is, in the first place, an allegory that promotes charity (though sometimes in a rather malevolent way); its author frequently cites the Fathers of the Church; it uses symbols, such as the Tree of Charity and Patience, that come from the patristic tradition; its meaning is occasionally so murky that one must invoke every sort of aid to understanding (not, I think, one of the poem's virtues); and, most important, it not only is based in large part upon biblical texts, but it frequently quotes the Scriptures, so that we should expect patristic interpretations to show up along with the passages they interpret. Here, if anywhere, is favorable soil for the plow drawn by the four oxen who ornament the title page of Huppé and Robertson's book, *Piers Plowman and Scriptural Tradition.* I am therefore the more disappointed by what the book itself contains.

Every one will recall the opening of the B-Text. On a May morning the speaker goes to sleep among the Malvern Hills and dreams that he sees before him

> . . . a towr on a toft, trieliche ymaked,
> A deep dale binethe, a dungeon therinne
> With deepe diches and derke, and dredful of sighte.
> A fair feeld ful of folk foond I therbitweene
> Of al manere of men, the mene and the riche,
> Worching and wandring as the world asketh.[9]

The critics begin their analysis of the poem with the statement, "In *Piers Plowman* the basic contrast between Jerusalem and Babylon is suggested at once by the dreamer's opening vision of the Tower of Truth, the Dungeon of Hell, and, in between, the Field of Folk."[10] This is certainly true, but nevertheless the phrasing of the statement causes me discomfort. Some one who had not read the poem carefully, or who had read only part of it, might very well get the idea that Langland habitually deals in terms of the compound patristic symbol Jerusalem vs. Babylon: the critics' phrasing surely suggests his easy familiarity with the patristic tradition. Yet the symbol here is the critics' and not Langland's. Indeed, while in his poem Jerusalem appears again and again with all its ancient symbolism upon it, Babylon is never hell, but just a foreign city. Instead of employing the patristic allegory of the two cities, the poet is content to give us two towers, one on a hillock, one in a dale, one fair, one ugly, but in any case towers of the kind that dotted the medieval English landscape. Since the critics fail to derive the towers from patristic sources, one might suggest that the poet had eschewed tradition for everyday reality, as poets often do: his own practical sensibility saw the great contrast as between the soaring watchtower (Watchman, tell us of the night) and the sullen keep (which is the night). And if this is going too far, one can at least, I think, say that the critics are guilty of smuggling in patristic symbolism at the very outset of their journey.

Let us proceed to their following sentences: "It is significant that the Folk are not assembled in an orderly pilgrimage toward the Tower [i.e., of Truth]: they are occupied with the world. . . . This situation represents the underlying problem in the poem. The folk of the world are preoccupied with worldly affairs, 'wandryng' in confusion." [11] Now this, I submit, is unwarranted intrusion upon the poem. It has not said or even hinted that the folk of the field are wrong in being occupied with the world; "worching and wandring" suggests that some of them are occupied with the world in the right way, some in the wrong way; but in either case, being in the world, they are necessarily concerned with it. The disapproval of this fact is not the poet's, but the critics'. St. Augustine might, in one of his more world-hating moments, have agreed with them, but he was not writing *Piers Plowman*. And indeed the critics suggest by their next sentence that in pursuing Augustine they have perhaps tripped on Langland. "But not all of them [the Folk] seem hopeless. The dreamer's attention is at once called to the hard working plowman." [12]

> Some putten hem to the plow, played ful selde,
> In setting and in sowing swonken ful harde,
> And wonnen that wastours with glutonye destroyeth.[13]

Now if I rightly understand the purport of the critics' remarks, these hard-working plowmen ought to be off on an orderly pilgrimage to the Tower of Truth, which, I take it, would make them somewhat better than merely not hopeless. And, of course, the image of life as a pilgrimage to Truth, or the Celestial City, is a time-honored one:

> This world nis but a thurghfare ful of wo,
> And we been pilgrimes passing to and fro.

Furthermore it is an image which Langland does, at times, invoke, but not here. For the poem is not considering just now the good man's life allegorically as a pilgrimage to Truth but literally as a life of productive work. The poem does indeed concern salvation, but it also recognizes the practical fact that salvation in the next world depends upon one's actions in this, and while it points the way to heaven it is also concerned with tidying up earth. The pilgrimage of the hard-working plowmen is their hard work. Later on in the poem Piers Plowman himself, like Huppé and Robertson, momentarily identifies the allegorical with the literal when he volunteers to leave off plowing and lead a pilgrimage to Truth; but Truth tells him in no uncertain terms to stay home and keep on plowing.[14] It is appropriate to notice here what St. Thomas repeats from St. Augustine about the fourfold interpretation of Scripture: "There is nothing darkly related in any part of Holy Writ which is not clearly revealed elsewhere." [15] In this case the critics have detected a dark pronouncement on the management of earthly affairs which the poem clearly controverts later. Plowmen by definition ought to plow.

Huppé and Robertson continue: "Unfortunately, the plowmen are accompanied by false plowmen, by persons who dress as plowmen through pride:" [16]

> And some putten hem to pride, apparailed hem therafter,
> In countenance of clothing comen disgised.[17]

While these lines directly follow the description of the plowmen, the only way one can turn the proud men they mention into false plowmen is by taking as the antecedent of the adverb *therafter* not the noun *pride,* which immediately precedes it, but the plowmen of three lines before. Now one may reasonably doubt that any one at all in the Middle Ages would, through pride, dress as a plowman, the lowest of the low; but this is as nothing to my doubt about the syntax which yields such an interpretation. It ought to be stated loudly that Middle English syntax, while it is different from that of Modern English and often far more colloquial, is wholly logical and bound by its own firm rules: it is not mere illiterate imprecision that permits one to read without regard for the niceties of correlation. Here the chances are about ninety-eight out of a hundred that *therafter* refers to pride; about one out of a hundred that it refers to *wastours,* which is the next closest antecedent; and about one out of a thousand that it refers to the plowmen. And certainly the natural sense is the best one: people filled with pride of worldly position dress up in fancy clothes. There are no false plowmen in the text: there are merely ornamental parasites contrasted with hard-working peasants.

The trouble is that the critics have been kidnapped by their preconceptions. Since they believe one of the most important themes of *Piers Plowman* to be that "the function of those in the *status praelatorum* has been usurped by certain members of the *status religiosorum*" [18]—the friars have taken over the duties of the secular clergy—they are anxious to have the poet develop this theme at once. For, as it now appears, the poem's plowmen are not just "simple peasants," [19] but represent, in the patristic tradition, "the true followers of the prelatical life." [20] Naturally, if the true plowmen are the displaced prelates, the poem ought at once to have mentioned the false plowmen—the friars—who have displaced them. We have seen how the text is made to do what it ought to have done. But the simple literal reading does not permit false plowmen. Furthermore, I am sure that the plowmen of the Prologue represent not prelates, but plowmen, men who are doing a necessary part of the dirty work exacted by this world. Having spent a good deal of time with the poem, I am aware that a plowman may be an image for a spiritual plowman, which is what Piers Plowman is or becomes in the course of the poem; but I hope that the first time I read the poem I had enough sensitivity to it to realize that the word *plowmen* was loaded, even without benefit of the Fathers. On the other hand, I do not think that I said at this point, "Hah, 'plowmen,' *id est, praelati.*" Nor do I think that any contemporary reader would have, though he might well have thought of all hard-working honest men, including priests. If he had said that, one cannot help wondering what he would have said when, a little later in the same catalogue of folk, he encounters parish priests. What in the world (or out of it) do they represent?

I shall pass over the remainder of Huppé and Robertson's interpretation of the catalogue of folk, merely pausing to observe that it seems wantonly to confuse the literal and the metaphorical. There are anchorites who are said to represent anchorites, merchants who are said to represent the whole laity, minstrels who are said to represent "those who use the goods of the world properly for the worship of God, who praise the Lord without desire for temporal reward"[21] (despite the fact that they "get gold with their glee"[22]), japers and janglers who are said to represent "those who profess the faith but do not work accordingly"; and finally beggars who are allowed to represent beggars, pardoners pardoners, priests priests, and bishops bishops. Any cryptographer who keeps forgetting his code and writing plain English is simply incompetent; I do not think Langland was incompetent or, for that matter, a cryptographer.

I shall conclude this part of my paper with one final analysis. Shortly after his vision of the Field of Folk the dreamer sees a vision of the founding of an earthly kingdom:

> Thanne cam ther a king, knighthood him ladde,
> Might of the comunes made him to regne;
> And thanne cam Kinde Wit, and clerkes he made,

For to conseille the king and the comune save.
The king and knighthood and clergye bothe
Casten that the comune sholde [hir comunes] finde.
The comune contreved of Kinde Wit craftes,
And for profit of alle the peple plowmen ordaigned,
To tilie and to travaile as trewe lif asketh.
The king and the comune and Kinde Wit the thridde
Shoop lawe and lewtee, eech [lif] to knowe his owene.[23]

I had always thought this an idealized picture of the political community. A king, supported by his knights and by the common people, counseled by clerks, assisted at every turn by Natural Intelligence, in order to serve the common profit and to fulfill the demands of a life of integrity, creates law and justice and assigns each component of the kingdom its place, so that every man should know his privileges and responsibilities. Apparently I was wrong, for the king's council

> did not consist of a representative body of his subjects; it was made up of clerks appointed by Kind Wit or *scientia.* The king, his barons, and the clergy, neglecting their responsibilities, decided that the commons must take care of themselves, so that the commons, also resorting to *scientia,* found it necessary to establish "plowmen." Together, the king and his commons, guided by *scientia,* formulated law and loyalty for the protection of private property, "eche man to knowe his owne."[24]

My errors had been many. I had not realized that representative government was a patristic ideal: I had thought it the ideal of a rather anti-patristic rationalism. I had not known that Kinde Wit was *scientia* and a villainously unreliable faculty: I had rather supposed the poet approved of it, since he very frequently couples it with Conscience; and Dunning and Hort exalt it almost to the position of modern "conscience" and "reason."[25] I had not been aware that king, knights, and clergy were neglecting their responsibility for taking care of the commons: for it had not occurred to me that the defenders and administrators of the realm ought to be out producing food, which is what I thought the verb *finden* meant and which I had assumed was a function of the commons, and specifically of plowmen. Nor had it become clear to me that the creation of law was a conspiracy to protect private property: I had thought that law and justice—which is what *lewtee* seems to mean—made possible social order, and that social order was desirable in this miserable world.

But my worst mistake was in connection with the last phrase of the passage, "each man [lif] to know his own," which I had once written was "the most significant phrase for understanding [the poet's] idea of earthly government."[26] I should have said "misunderstanding." For the two critics write of it: "That this is not a proper goal is evident from I Cor. 10.24: *Nemo quod suum est quaerat.*"[27] Let no man seek his own. They go on, quite correctly, to define the seeking of one's own as cupidity, the opposite of charity, and hence the negative side of the principle which, according to them, is the theme of all medieval literature.

You may remember that at the end of the Rat Parliament in the B-Prologue a little mouse taunts the rats with their failure to bell the cat and offers the cold consolation that it was a bad idea in the first place. The mouse ends his speech with the line,

> Forthy eech a wis wight I warne, wite wel his owene.

Therefore I warn each wise wight to wit well his own. Needless to say, under the scrutiny of the critics this turns out to be a very wicked little rodent indeed, counseling the rats, like Belial, to slothful ease, or, like Mammon, to seeking wealth and heeding not St. Paul's injunction. But the truth is that he is no more telling the rats to seek their own than law is encouraging men to seek their own in the earlier passage. I once wrote that "without risk of error, one may add the word *place* or *part* in order to make the phrase meet the requirements of modern idiom: each man, and therefore each class, should know and keep his own place." [28] Furthermore, I remain persuaded that this is what the phrase means, and that knowledge of one's own place in the world is a cardinal point in medieval theorizing of the most idealistic kind, that it is a principle upon which all order in this world depends: I'll bet it is in the Fathers. The truth is that Huppé and Robertson have on two occasions mistranslated Middle English to make a point that is not only entirely foreign to the poem's but directly opposed to it and disproved by other passages within the poem. They have made an ideal state a wicked one; and they have made of a poet counseling forbearance a revolutionary. In order to do this, they have taken first Middle English *knowen,* then *witen,* as the equivalents of Latin *quaerere;* they have made knowing the same as seeking. Once again it is relevant to quote St. Thomas on scriptural interpretation: "The spiritual sense is always based upon the literal sense, and proceeds from it."[29] The literal sense of *to know* is "to know."

It seems to me that the failure which the two critics suffer with regard to the literal sense in the beginning of their analysis is repeated again and again as the analysis proceeds. It is patently unfair to condemn a whole work on the basis of a few pages, but I do not consider the sample uncharacteristic. The authors seem constantly to be contorting the text to find the message they want to find. This tendency reaches a kind of open confirmation in their discussion of the meaning of the protagonist's name, Will. After pointing out, I think rather suggestively, that Will, like the human will, "moves between the opposites of willfulness and charity," they go on to observe: "Because the poet has been successful as a poet, he has created in Will so appealingly human a character that through interest in him many have lost sight of the fact that Will is merely a device by means of which the poet may set off the actual against the ideal in the poem and so develop his major theme."[30] It is fair to read this as saying that because the poet has been a good poet, he has been a poor teacher, and one might work out the proposition, the better the poet, the worse the teacher, and vice versa. Ultimately one has the poem going in one direction and its teaching going in the opposite. Under these circumstances I should prefer to follow the poem rather than outsiders who are telling me what it means to be saying.

There are, of course, good things in Huppé and Robertson's book. But curiously enough, these are in general not concerned with patristic exegesis, but are the insights of two excellent minds that have thought long and hard about the poem. The poet himself, when he is following patristic tradition, tends to explain his use of symbols in such a way that a reader ignorant of the tradition can understand them from the text—though of course knowledge of the tradition will enhance the reader's appreciation. Thus when the dreamer meets some one called Abraham representing faith, the first thing that Abraham says is, "I am Faith." [31] A character named Hope appears only to say at once that he has been given a "maundement" upon the Mount of Sinai.[32] The most heavily patristic passage in the poem, that describing the Tree of Charity,[33] is also well-glossed by the poet—rather better glossed by him, I think, than by Huppé and Robertson. Scholars must, indeed, be grateful to the critics for the information they provide about the patristic background, a field in which they are enormously learned. But I can think of little that they say on the subject which the poem does not say equally well. And when, as in the passages I have analyzed, they substitute a remote allegory for the easy sense, they are letting their desire to show patristic influence override the simple demands of Middle English.

Having shown what I think to be a failure with regard to the *littera* of a medieval poem, let me turn to what I consider a failure with regard to the *sensus*. The *Nun's Priest's Tale* has always been one of Chaucer's most popular and at the same time most elusive works: one is apt to come away from this feast feeling that one has been abundantly fed, but one is not sure on what kind of food. No simple critical formula explains the reader's delight in the poem, which has so little plot and such enormous rhetorical dilation. Since the scholarly mind naturally abhors a vacuum of this sort, it is inevitable that a number of attempts should be made to show that the little plot is weighty enough to compensate for and even to overbalance the infinite expansiveness of the narrator. Of several attempts of this sort more or less concerned with the patristic tradition, I shall choose that of Mortimer Donovan, since his is the most specifically patristic.[34]

According to Donovan, the morality of the *Nun's Priest's Tale*—or sermon, as he prefers to call it—emerges only if one understands the patristic significance of the personages concerned. The poor widow who owns Chauntecleer and his several wives is the Church;[35] the fox is either the Devil or a heretic, or rather, both;[36] the rooster, originally a symbol of alertness,[37] comes, in the course of the analysis, to represent the alert Christian, though strictly speaking he should represent an alert priest; Dame Pertelote is, of course, woman, whose counsel Chauntecleer, through lechery, has listened to "against his own superior judgment."[38] The climax of the action in which these figures share is, according to the critic,

> reached as Chauntecleer rides uncomfortably on the fox's back. Since Christian hope extends to the last, the once uxorious Chauntecleer now turns for divine aid against an adversary as powerful as Daun Russell, and, with all the alertness of his celebrated nature, he begs help. He knows with Chaucer's Parson that "for as muchel as the devil fighteth agayns a man moore by queyntise and by sleighte than by strengthe, therfor men shal withstonden hym by wit and by resoun and by discrecioun." . . . So, begging divine help, he devises a plan which shows a return of reason.[39]

And so the alert Christian defeats the Devil-heretic in the nick of time.

There is no way of proving that the widow does not represent the Church—unless, of course, we apply to the tale St. Augustine's and St. Thomas's stricture that nothing is darkly said in one place that is not clearly revealed elsewhere. But I doubt that the fox represents the Devil or that Chauntecleer represents the alert Christian, not with seven wives. There were, if I may say so, foxes long before there were devils, and roosters were crowing off the hours long before Christians heard them. One might say that if there were no Devil a poultry-keeping farmer would have invented one in order to describe a fox, so that we hardly need Rabanus Maurus to explain the similarity between fox and devil, any more than we need Hugh of St. Victor to tell us that the cock in his hourly crowing makes a good natural example of attention to duty.[40] What we have here in poetic (or barnyard) terms is a devilish fox-villain and a conscientious, if foolish, rooster-hero. I am willing to accept the premise that Pertelote represents woman, though I think it's unkind of the critic to repeat the Nun's Priest's slander that Chauntecleer took her advice, something the Nun's Priest suggests in his eagerness to blame Chauntecleer's misfortune on anything and everything except Chauntecleer. Actually, Pertelote had advised certain medicines, but Chauntecleer had defied them, heroically, just as he defied dreams: Adam Rooster was at least able to resist eating Eve Hen's hellebore, and thereby maintained a kind of integrity, if a prideful and lecherous one.

On first reading Donovan's criticism I thought he had inadvertently left out Chauntecleer's prayer for divine aid—which I couldn't recall—for all he quotes is Chauntecleer's speech to the fox:

. . . Sire, if that I were as ye,
Yet sholde I sayn, *as wis God helpe me,*
'Turneth again, ye proude cherles alle!
A verray pestilence upon you falle!'

Then I realized that the words "as wis God helpe me," as surely as God help me, were italicized,[41] and were, indeed, the prayer that Chauntecleer uttered "with all the alertness of his celebrated nature." But even this crumb is not really available: the prayer qualifies the apodasis of a contrary-to-fact condition, in a position safely removed from the actual Chauntecleer; and it is, indeed, not a prayer at all, but an oath of which Chaucer's Parson would not have approved.

Even if one were to accept the allegorical interpretation of this tale I cannot see that much has, critically speaking, been gained. If one connects things up with a specific Christian doctrine one does, to be sure, introduce a kind of weightiness into the discussion, but in this case it seems a deadweight of which the poem were better relieved. I must say, in all seriousness, that if the *sententia* of the *Nun's Priest's Tale,* the quality which justifies our reading the tale, is that the alert Christian with God's help can thwart the Devil-heretic, then Chaucer has let us down with a thud. But I do not think he has. At the end of his critique, Donovan tells us that "the identity of the cock and fox is almost lost behind what Professor Kittredge calls this 'preacher's illustrative anecdote, enormously developed until it swallows up the sermon.' "[42] This seems a little like running out into the streets shouting "Eureka!" only to discover that one has neglected to dress; for the fact is that the little anecdote on which the exegesis depends is only one tiny grain of wheat in an intolerable deal of chaff, and if it contains Chaucer's main point then he is guilty of the most horrid misproportioning. But one ought to trust the statistics of great poetry rather than those of critics, and any interpretation of a poem that ignores the bulk of it is likely to be wrong: a medieval teacher would have warned us to heed the *sensus* before extracting the *sententia.*

The *Nun's Priest's Tale* does have a real point, a serious point, and a better point than the one I reject, and it lies where one should expect to find it, in the enormous rhetorical elaboration of the telling. For rhetoric here is regarded as the inadequate defense that mankind erects against an inscrutable reality; rhetoric enables man at best to regard himself as a being of heroic proportions—like Achilles, or like Chauntecleer—and at worst to maintain the last sad vestiges of his dignity (as a rooster Chauntecleer is carried in the fox's mouth, but as a hero he rides on his back); rhetoric enables man to find significance both in his desires and in his fate, and to pretend to himself that the universe takes him seriously. And rhetoric has a habit, too, of collapsing in the presence of simple common sense. Chauntecleer is not an alert Christian; he is mankind trying to adjust the universe to his own specifications and failing—though not, I am happy to say, fatally. Donovan assumes that Chauntecleer has been cured of his uxoriousness—perhaps he is going to retire into voluntary widowhood. I am less sanguine. I fear he is going to go on behaving as the roosters and men of Western civilization have always behaved, preserving their dignity by artificial respiration and somewhat against the odds. In short, the fruit of the *Nun's Priest's Tale* is its chaff.[43]

I shall conclude with one final analysis of patristic exegesis,

Robertson's interpretation of the little lyric "Maiden in the Moor."[44] In this poem we have the barest of literal statements and almost no *sensus* at all; one must proceed directly from the letter to the *sententia*. The poem is short; therefore I quote it entire:

Maiden in the moor lay,
  In the moor lay,
Sevenight ful, sevenight ful;
Maiden in the moor lay,
  In the moor lay,
Sevenightes ful and a day.

Wel [i.e., good] was hir mete.
  What was hir mete?
The primerole and the—
The primerole and the—
Wel was hir mete.
  What was hir mete?
The primerole and the violet.

Wel was hir dring.
  What was hir dring?
The chelde water of the—
The chelde water of the—
Wel was hir dring.
  What was hir dring?
The chelde water of the welle-spring.

Wel was hir bowr.
  What was hir bowr?

The rede rose and the—
The rede rose and the—
Wel was hir bowr.
  What was hir bowr?
The rede rose and the lilye flowr.[45]

Of this charming little piece Robertson writes:

> On the surface, although the poem is attractive, it cannot be said to make much sense. Why should a maiden lie on a moor for seven nights and a day? And if she did, why should she eat primroses and violets? Or again, how does it happen that she has a bower of lilies and roses on the moor? The poem makes perfectly good sense, however, if we take note of the figures and signs in it. The number seven indicates life on earth, but life in this instance went on at night, or before the Light of the World dawned. The day is this light, or Christ, who said, "I am the day." And it appears appropriately after seven nights, or, as it were, on the count of eight, for eight is also a figure of Christ. The moor is the wilderness of the world under the Old Law before Christ came. The primrose is not a Scriptural sign, but a figure of fleshly beauty. We are told three times that the primrose was the food of this maiden, and only after this suspense are we also told that she ate or embodied the violet, which is a Scriptural sign of humility. The maiden drank the cool water of God's grace, and her bower consisted of the roses of martyrdom or charity and the lilies of purity with which late medieval and early Renaissance artists sometimes adorned

pictures of the Blessed Virgin Mary, and, indeed, she is the Maiden in the Moor. . . .[46]

I cannot find that the poem, as a poem, makes any more "sense" after exegesis than it did before, and I think it makes rather more sense as it stands than the critic allows it. Maidens in poetry often receive curiously privileged treatment from nature, and readers seem to find the situation agreeable. From the frequency with which it has been reprinted it seems that the "Maiden in the Moor" must have offered many readers a genuine poetic experience even though they were without benefit of the scriptural exegesis. I do not think that most of them would find it necessary to ask the questions of the poem that Robertson has asked; indeed, it seems no more legitimate to inquire what the maiden was doing in the moor than it would be to ask Wordsworth's Lucy why she did not remove to a more populous environment where she might experience a greater measure of praise and love. In each case the poetic *donnée* is the highly primitive one which exposes an innocent woman to the vast, potentially hostile, presumably impersonal forces of nature; and the Middle English lyric suggests the mystery by which these forces are, at times, transmuted into something more humane, even benevolent, by their guardianship of the innocent maiden. The poetic sense is not such as necessarily to preclude allegory, and I shouldn't be surprised if medieval readers often thought of the Virgin as they read the poem, not because they knew the symbols and signs, but because the Virgin is the paramount innocent maiden of the Christian tradition: such suggestivity is one of poetry's principal functions. Robertson's hard-and-fast, this-sense-or-no-sense allegory, however, seems to me so well-concealed and, when explicated, so unrevealing that it can be considered only disappointing if not entirely irrelevant. The function of allegory that is worth the literary critic's attention (as opposed to cryptography, which is not) cannot be to conceal, but is to reveal, and I simply do not believe that medieval poets veiled their poems in order to hide their pious message from heretics and unbelievers. In allegory the equation is not merely *a* equals *b,* the literal statement reanalyzed equals the suggested meaning, but is something more like *a* plus *b* equals *c,* the literal statement plus the meaning it suggests yield an ultimate meaning that is an inextricable union of both. Patristically the primrose may be a figure of fleshy beauty, but actually (and the actual is what poetry is made of) it is one of the commonest of the lovely flowers which nature in its benevolent aspect lavishes upon mankind and, in this case, all-benevolent lavishes upon the maiden of the moor. Robertson asks the question "Why should she eat primroses?" I hope that if I answer "Because she was hungry," it will not be said of me that a primrose by the river's brim a yellow primrose was to him, and it was nothing more.

I said at the beginning of this paper that I did not know of any valid theoretical objection to patristic criticism. I do, however, object to a procedure which substitutes for the art of the poet the learning or good intentions of the reader. Reading a poem intelligently is, I believe, one of the hardest things on earth to do:

> Humankind cannot bear very much reality,

and I believe that great poetic art offers something very close to an ultimate reality. In order to read it well one has to put oneself into the impossible position of having all one's wits and faculties about one, ready to spring into activity at the first summons; yet, like hunting dogs, they must not spring before they are summoned; and only those that are summoned must spring; and the summons must come from the poem. To maintain oneself in this state of relaxed tension is frightfully fatiguing, and any serious reader will, I am sure, want to rest a good deal. This is fortunate for scholarship, since such activities as source study, investigation of historical context, philology, editing, and patristic exegesis are salubrious vacations from the awful business of facing a poem directly. For a good many people the interest implicit in such studies and the fun of them will become more important than the poems themselves, and this is understandable; and the activities I have mentioned and many more are as necessary and as honorable as literary criticism. I look forward myself to a year when the many incidental problems of editing *Piers Plowman* will, I hope, constantly distract me from the effort of understanding its meaning. But these activities are not the same as literary criticism, and none of them should be permitted to replace an interpretation of the poem arising from the poem. At certain periods source study, philology, historical orientation, and even some of the techniques of the new criticism have tended to obliterate the meaning of the poems with which they have associated themselves. It seems to me that patristic criticism is operating under a categorical imperative to do the same thing.

Robertson concludes his English Institute paper on patristic criticism with the remark that literature, "regarded historically" —by which he means patristically—"can provide the food of wisdom as well as more transient aesthetic satisfactions."[47] It is here that my disagreement with him becomes absolute. I do not feel that the effect that the poems of Chaucer and Langland and other poets have upon me is mere transient aesthetic satisfaction. I believe that a great work of art provides the reader with the food of wisdom because it is a great work of art. If this food is not specific Christian doctrine, I console myself that it emanates from a humane tradition that is as old as Western civilization and that Christianity has done much to preserve.

THE DEFENSE

R. E. Kaske

INTERPRETATION of the Vulgate Bible occupied a central place in the intellectual life of the Middle Ages. Its results are preserved systematically in the abundant commentaries on the Vulgate itself, as well as in various encyclopedic collections of exegetical commonplaces; they are embodied piecemeal in many other traditional Christian forms, such as sermons and homilies, the Latin hymns and sequences, the liturgy of the Church, and the pictorial arts. In the course of the Middle Ages, the allegorizing technique which formed an important part of biblical exegesis was increasingly extended to non-biblical material as well—notably by the mythographers and by encyclopedists like Rabanus Maurus, Thomas of Cantimpré, John of San Geminiano, and Pierre Bersuire, who allegorize also phenomena drawn directly from the natural sciences.[1]

The whole of this sprawling exegetical tradition, it seems to me, can make broadly two kinds of contribution to our understanding of medieval literature. The first, which has been recognized to some extent in modern scholarship, is that of explaining the medieval interpretations underlying obvious biblical quotations or allusions. A second contribution—potentially greater, though it has been relatively little exploited in the study of medieval English literature—derives from the role of the entire exegetical tradition as a sort of massive index to the traditional meanings and associations of most medieval Christian imagery. I refer, of course, not to the venerable pastime of source-hunting, but to the close analysis of the traditional associations which such imagery usually brings with it into literary works, and the interpretation of whatever artistic use has been made of them. At the risk of introducing a note of tedium into a hitherto attractive controversy, the main part of my paper will demonstrate the interpretation of exegetical imagery and allusion by a series of examples from Langland and Chaucer; I have included fuller documentation for most of them in articles either in print or awaiting publication.[2]

Before settling down to cases, however, let me clarify a few of my own premises, which may disagree at some points with those of other scholars whatever their attitudes toward exegetical interpretation. There is, it seems, a certain emotional objection to this exegetical approach, in the belief that any such concentration on what are loosely thought of as "religious" allusions must regiment all medieval writers into a row of humorless proselytizers, preaching a monotonous gospel to later emancipated generations. Without denying the fundamental didacticism of most medieval literature, I think there is an important distinction to be made here. Even in basically didactic works, "religious" imagery or allusion need not be employed in simple evangelic frenzy, like a series of vendors' cries; one expects as a matter of course that a civilized Christian writer will use it with objective artistry, as a meaningful, evocative, and perhaps unique image for what he is trying to express. Particularly would this be true in a civilization which seems to have distinguished much less sharply between "religious" and "secular" thought than does our own. So used, I do not see that exegetical imagery is more limited in its range of possible effects than imagery or allusion of any other kind. If this principle is sound, however, it has an important converse application: The interpreter of such imagery must not be content to reduce it indiscriminately to the most inclusive and uniform terms, but must analyze carefully its precise meanings in its particular contexts. Not every exegetical image or allusion is most fruitfully interpreted by direct recourse to *charitas* and *cupiditas,* accurate though the formula may be as universalizing commentary.

Another objection sometimes made to the exegetical approach is that few medieval writers—particularly fourteenth-century laymen, like Chaucer—would have had so much knowledge of biblical exegesis; and that in any case their audience could have understood few allusions to it. If I may invoke a few truisms: It is a notorious fact that a poet needs considerably less systematized information than do—ideally, anyway—the scholars of a later day who pursue him, since where he chooses to lead, we must follow; we may spend years in accumulating and sifting out what he has picked up painlessly in a conversation, a sermon, or an evening's casual reading. I suppose it is equally obvious that poets do not always write to be wholly understood by readers or hearers less sophisticated than themselves, or to be wholly understood with ease by any audience; one might profitably ask, in fact, whether the use of exegetical allusion really involves a greater intrinsic improbability, or creates a more demanding kind of literature, than does the allusion of Donne or Eliot. There remains, as a final problem, that abstraction about whom we admittedly know next to nothing—the "sophisticated fourteenth-century English audience." Now according to our own common experience of human capacities for informal knowledge, surely no one would deny that such an audience *might* have been aware of a fairly large body of unsystematized exegetical lore. On the one hand, I know of no concrete evidence that has ever been brought forward for the absence of this awareness; while on the other hand there is some strong indirect evidence for its presence: for example, Chaucer's casual mention of Peter Riga's great exegetical poem the *Aurora;* the freedom with which Langland, Chaucer, and others employ references to glossing and the general apparatus of biblical commentary, often as the vehicle of metaphor; and, most significant of all, the thousands of obviously exegetical allusions to be found in medieval art, medieval homiletic literature, and the medieval liturgy including the hymns and sequences.

Such external arguments—including even the valuable supporting evidence of medieval poetic theory, so far as it can be ascertained—must in themselves be ultimately inconclusive; but they do imply that if we can find convincing and important examples of exegetical allusion in medieval literature, we need not shut our eyes to them in the simple faith that they could not possibly be there. The normal discipline of scholarly argument, of course, demands that exegetical interpretation of an individual figure or allusion be supported by well-documented parallels from the exegetical literature itself, somehow embracing enough peculiar features that to consider them accidental would outrage probability. More extended exegetical allusion in a given work must be supported by an accumulation of parallels large enough, or by a pattern complex enough, that to consider it accidental would outrage probability. But if this is so, the same scholarly discipline seems to dictate that the only conclusive evidence for the absence of exegetical allusion in a work—a few extraordinary cases apart—will be a demonstrable absence of such parallels.

Like almost any new line of scholarly inquiry, the exegetical approach to medieval literature has before it inevitably several large problems, some of them extremely complex. For example, to what extent do medieval writers actually draw their material, their governing outlooks, and their means of literary expression, from the exegetical tradition? What theory, if any, underlies their use of it? Where it does seem to be consistently used, to what extent does it produce a connected level of meaning beyond the literal, and to what extent merely a number of separate allusions? To what extent, if any, do medieval writers employ creatively the famous "four levels" of biblical exegesis? If a substantial literary use of the exegetical tradition can be recognized, what major channels made it a part of the cultural repertory of medieval writers and their audiences? On most of these questions there would still be considerable disagreement, even among scholars convinced of the general validity of the discipline itself. My own opinion is that although they are obviously important questions, they are not the most immediately profitable ones; I would suggest, in fact, that these are the very questions scholarship is not yet equipped to answer. What we need first is a really prodigious amount of minute, systematic research centered on individual medieval works, with the immediate aim of showing the precise contributions made by the exegetical tradition to the meaning of descriptive details, figures of speech, characters, limited passages, and so on.

For no medieval English work that I know of has this basic research ever been done, though a bold beginning has been made by D. W. Robertson and B. F. Huppé in *Piers Plowman and Scriptural Tradition*. Reviewers have pointed out serious errors and weaknesses in their work, for the most part justly. Rather less acknowledgment has been made of their positive contributions: the number of passages and details for which they convincingly show an exegetical background, and the consequent attention they have called to the large questions already mentioned. For our present discussion, however, the most significant weakness of their book is its tendency to proceed from general assumption to the explanation of particulars, instead of vice versa; the resulting paradox is that it does not make intensive enough use of the exegetical tradition which is its distinctive tool. This weakness, I take it, grows out of a situation not altogether under the authors' control—that is, lack of the solid foundation of preliminary scholarship referred to earlier, on which their own comprehensive interpretation could be partly based. An interpretation of *Piers Plowman,* supported by whatever is most relevant from the immense and still imperfectly conquered exegetical tradition, is hardly a task to be begun *ex nihilo* by two scholars and brought to perfection within the covers of a single book; if it were, the book would be one we might all have to get a year's grant to read. In this important way, the work of Robertson and Huppé is like a pinnacle without a sufficiently wide base. And except for their own contributions, the lack that existed when they wrote exists today. It seems less accurate, then, to say that the approach to *Piers Plowman* by way of the exegetical tradition has failed, than that it has not yet been painstakingly tried. Hence, in part, the examples which follow.

My first passage is a single extended simile from *Piers Plowman,* occurring within Will's first inner dream, in a speech uncertainly assigned in the B-Text, in a discussion of poverty:

And alle the wyse that euere were . by auȝte I can aspye,
Preysen pouerte for best lyf . if pacience it folwe,
And bothe bettere and blisseder . by many-folde than ricchesse.
Al though it be soure to suffre . there cometh swete after;
As on a walnot with-oute . is a bitter barke,
And after that bitter barke . (be the shelle aweye),
Is a kirnelle of conforte . kynde to restore;
So is, after, pouerte or penaunce . pacientlyche ytake.
For it maketh a man to haue mynde in gode . and a grete wille
To wepe and to wel bydde . wher-of wexeth mercy,
Of which Cryst is a kirnelle . to conforte the soule.

(B-Text XI.247–57)

This figure is derived from medieval interpretations of two biblical verses: Canticles 6.10, "I descended into the garden of nuts"; and the miraculous production of almonds or nuts by Aaron's rod in Numbers 17.8. Both verses have a variety of interpretations, all beginning with the ancient division of the nut into bitter hull, hard shell, and sweet kernel, found in Philo and Pliny. Langland's figure on poverty blends together two of the most common of these interpretations. The general pattern of the first may be illustrated from the twelfth-century comment of the Cistercian Thomas of Citeaux, on Canticles 6.10:

> . . . just as the nut has a most bitter hull and is girded about with a most hard shell, and when the harsh-tasting and hard parts have been taken away a most sweet fruit is found, so all the chastisement and labor of restraint by which Holy Church is exercised seems bitter indeed while it is present, but in the future brings forth most sweet fruit.

Later commentators apply the same pattern to those who patiently bear external hardships but have the sweetness of divine consolation within; and to those from whom harsh lives have called forth compassion, mercy, and true devotion.

Langland's final reference to Christ as a "kernel" touches on a second traditional interpretation of the two biblical verses, which makes the nut or almond signify Christ Himself—as, for example, in Adam of St. Victor's great Christmas sequence *Splendor Patris et figura,* where the hull and the shell are associated with Christ's physical sufferings during the Crucifixion, the kernel with the hidden sweetness of His divinity for mankind. In uniting these two traditional exegeses of the nut, then, Langland has utilized their spiritually meaningful common ground: the interpretations of the kernel, in which the sweetness that follows tribulation and the sweetness of internal devotion are both merged with the sweetness of Christ—probably to be thought of, accordingly, both as man's eternal reward and as man's internal dweller and counselor. Seen thus, in its exegetical context, the figure gains not only in the purposefulness of its own inner structure, but also in the metaphysical allusiveness that can distinguish medieval religious poetry at its best.

Such small and clear-cut uses of exegetical imagery are frequent in *Piers Plowman.* Leaving this specimen to stand for them all, I proceed to more complex examples. A passage which so far as I know has never been interpreted, either within itself or in its relation to the rest of the poem, is the abrupt speech of Book just before the Harrowing of Hell:

Thanne was there a wiȝte . with two brode eyen,
Boke hiȝte that beupere . a bolde man of speche.
"By godes body," quod this Boke . "I wil bere witnesse,
That tho this barne was ybore . there blased a sterre,
That alle the wyse of this worlde . in o witte acordeden,
That such a barne was borne . in Bethleem citee,
That mannes soule sholde saue . and synne destroye.
And alle the elementz," quod the Boke . "her-of bereth witnesse.
That he was god that al wrouȝte . the walkene firste shewed;
Tho that weren in heuene . token *stella comata,*
And tendeden hir as a torche . to reuerence his birthe;
The lyȝte folwed the lorde . in-to the lowe erthe.
The water witnessed that he was god . for he went on it;
Peter the apostel . parceyued his gate,
And as he went on the water . wel hym knewe, and seyde,
Iube me venire ad te super aquas.
And lo! how the sonne gan louke . her liȝte in her-self,
Whan she seye hym suffre . that sonne and se made!
The erthe for heuynesse . that he wolde suffre,
Quaked as quykke thinge . and al biquashte the roche!
Lo! helle miȝte nouȝte holde . but opened tho god tholed,
And lete oute Symondes sones . to seen hym hange on rode.
And now shal Lucifer leue it . thowgh hym loth thinke;
For *Gygas* the geaunt . with a gynne engyned
To breke and to bete doune . that ben aȝeines Iesus.

And I, Boke, wil be brent . but Iesus rise to lyue,
In alle myȝtes of man . and his moder gladye,
And conforte al his kynne . and out of care brynge,
And al the Iuwen Ioye . vnioignen and vnlouken;
And but thei reuerencen his rode . and his resurexioun,
And bileue on a newe lawe . be lost lyf and soule."

(B-Text xviii.228–57)

Let us begin by recalling that from a Christian point of view, Book's speech falls within the most suspenseful brief period in human history: the time between Christ's apparent defeat by Death, and the conclusive vindication of Christianity by the Harrowing of Hell and the Resurrection. More specifically, the speech stands about as squarely as possible between the period of the Old Law and that of the New, introduced as it is between the completion of the Atonement with the death of Christ, and its first fruits as manifested in the Harrowing of Hell. The Debate of the Daughters of God immediately preceding it presents a conflict of claims incompatible under the Old Law; the Harrowing of Hell which immediately follows is a dramatization of the reconciling of these claims, and of the change to the conditions of the New Law. In accord with this crucial placing, the speech of Book is designed not only as literal comment on the career of Christ and its climax in the present stupendous world-moment, but also as a kind of double-surfaced mirror reflecting the essential truth of both past and future—just as, according to medieval commentary, the essential truth of both past and future is reflected in the letter of the New Testament. This controlling pattern is developed primarily by the use of themes taken from the exegetical tradition.

The most obvious of these exegetical themes is Book's long account of the witnessing elements, extending from line 235 through line 248. This whole theme is itself a homiletic interpretation of part of the second chapter of Matthew, attached primarily to the feast of the Epiphany though sometimes to the Crucifixion. In the West, it is found in Augustine and in a famous pseudo-Augustinian sermon on the Creed, but it receives its definitive formulation in a homily by Gregory the Great on Matthew 2.1–12, delivered on the day of Epiphany:

> Indeed all the elements bore witness that their author had come. For (so that I may say something of them in human terms) the heavens acknowledged Him to be God, because straightway they sent a star. The sea acknowledged it, because it offered itself to be trodden upon by His footsteps. The earth acknowledged it, because when He died it trembled. The sun acknowledged it, because it hid the rays of its light. Rocks and walls acknowledged it, because at the time of His death they were cleft. Hell acknowledged it, because it yielded up dead those whom it held.

This passage is incorporated into the lections for Matins on the feast of the Epiphany; it is also repeated more or less closely in the Old English *Christ*-poem, and in a long series of medieval sermons and homilies on the Epiphany, including an English metrical homily of the fourteenth century.

In adapting this theme as a basic part of Book's speech, Langland is obviously utilizing both its inevitable correspondences to the Gospel account, and its strong motif of literal, physical testimony, in order to establish Book's role as primarily the witness-bearing "letter" of the New Testament. Moreover, Book's extended opening reference to the familiar Epiphany-motif of the star of Bethlehem (ll. 231 ff.) and his extended closing reference to the wonders surrounding the Crucifixion (ll. 243 ff.) seem to throw particular emphasis on these two major traditional contexts of the witnessing elements theme—one standing near the beginning and the other at the end of Christ's earthly career. And these traditional contexts of the theme, in turn, further emphasize the role of Book's speech as the point of transition between Old Law and New: The Epiphany, despite its origins, traditionally celebrates the visit of the Magi, always interpreted as the first manifestation of Christ to the Gentiles, and often including a reproach to the Jews for their blindness to the promised Redeemer; the Crucifixion, as the completion of the Atonement, marks the final abolition of the Old Law and the beginning of the New.

A second major exegetical theme in the speech is based on Psalm 18.1–8, unanimously explained in medieval commentary as a prophecy of the life of Christ. In line 250, "*Gygas* the geaunt" is a clear reference to the giant of Psalm 18.6, "Exsultavit ut gigas ad currendam viam," who is identified with Christ by practically every commentator from Ambrose in the fourth century to Nicolas of Lyra in the fourteenth—a figure occasionally supported by manuscript illustration, and particularly common in the Latin hymns and sequences. With this allusion as a basis, we may see a probable further connection between Book's opening account of the star of Bethlehem (ll. 231 ff.) and Psalm 18.1, "The heavens expound the glory of God," often explained by commentators as a prophecy of the star; and a similar connection between Book's closing remark about the conversion of the

Jews to the New Law (ll. 256–57) and Psalm 18.8, "The law of the Lord is immaculate, converting souls," often explained as a prophecy of the New Law.

It is primarily through these two exegetical themes that Langland develops the Janus-like pattern already proposed for Book's speech. The significance of the literal present—that is, the change from Old Law to New—is emphasized by the theme of the witnessing elements, plus its traditional associations with the change from Old Law to New and from Jew to Gentile. The meaningful past—that is, the Old Law—is reflected by the allusions to Psalm 18, one of the most prominent Old Testament foreshadowings of Christianity. The future—that is, the time of the New Law proper—is directly foretold by the rest of Book's speech (ll. 252 ff.), with its further emphasis on the invalidating of the Old Law; a possible important allusion to Joachistic prophetic commentary in this final part of the speech is too doubtful and complex for discussion here. To the entire pattern, one might add the sharp division of Book's speech into a record of miracles and a prophecy, dramatizing a common exegetical statement of the two basic means by which the Scriptures present their testimony.

If this interpretation is generally sound, the speech of Book emerges from its apparent chaos as one of the most originally conceived, intellectually controlled, and compact passages of allusion in *Piers Plowman* or elsewhere. Broader implications can be found in this governing design, such as its probable relation to the Book of Scripture and the Book of Nature. More to our present point, however, the pattern is filled out by lesser exegetical details; as a single example, let us glance back to the sketch of Book himself in the first two lines of the passage. Book's two eyes seem to represent most immediately an antithesis to the traditional blindness of the Jews and their Law—a common exegetical theme, actually found along with that of the witnessing elements in the lections for Matins on Epiphany. Further likely connotations drawn from Scriptural exegesis are the two Testaments themselves; the different senses in which Scripture is to be understood; and particularly the relationship of the New Testament to both past and future, following interpretations of Apocalypse 4.6 like that of the ninth-century commentator Smaragdus: "The four animals signify the four Gospels: they are full of eyes in front because they preach concerning future judgment; they are full of eyes behind, because they give testimony concerning the Old Testament. . . ." Book's boldness of speech (l. 229) echoes a New Testament ideal familiar in the Acts and the Pauline epistles. I read it as a particular allusion to Romans 10.20–21, concerning the boldness of Isaias in prophesying the faith of the Gentiles by contrast with the incredulity of the Jews—a passage unanimously interpreted as a statement of the change in Laws and in the comparative importance of Jew and Gentile, already outlined as the thematic center of Book's speech.

The exegetical tradition can also be fruitfully applied to some of the difficult passages mentioning Piers himself. A good example is the well known allusion by Anima in the B-Text, in a passage referring to Charity:

> There-fore by coloure ne by clergye . knowe shaltow hym neuere,
> Noyther thorw wordes ne werkes . but thorw wille one.
> And that knoweth no clerke . ne creature in erthe,
> But Piers the Plowman . *Petrus, id est, Christus.* (xv.203–6)

Though modern scholars seem generally agreed that Piers here is to be identified primarily with St. Peter and the prelacy, the precise rationale of *Petrus, id est, Christus* has been left rather mysterious. One solution has been to refer, a little uncomfortably, to Konrad Burdach, who cites "an old, much ramified speculation"—undocumented—that the Apostle Peter is "a source of life for the community of human souls who seek God."[3] Whatever Burdach may have had in mind, I do not think we need go so far afield for an explanation. To begin with, the gloss "Petra, id est Christus" is almost a refrain in biblical commentary—connected as it is not only with Moses' striking the rock in Exodus 17.6 and Paul's famous interpretation of it in I Corinthians 10.4, but with a number of other familiar passages in which the rock signifies Christ. Langland's *Petrus, id est, Christus,* then, is really a metaphor—or, if we like, an allusive adaptation—using as its vehicle a recognizable cliché of biblical exegesis. *Petrus* (the Apostle and through him the prelacy) *stands for Christ* in the visible history of the Church Militant, just as *petra* (the rock) "stands for Christ" in the text of Scripture. The topical connection between *Petrus* and *petra* is of course found in Christ's words, "Thou art Peter, and upon this rock I will build my Church" (Matthew 16.18), consistently interpreted as the establishment of the papacy. In other words, Langland is extending Christ's own pun on *Petrus* and *petra* to embrace also the great exegetical commonplace of Christ Himself as *petra,* an extension already familiar in commentaries on the verse.

But if this is so, what is the precise relevance of the figure to the theme of its immediate context—that is, to the surpassing need for charity, with particular reference to the clergy? The key seems clearly to lie in the interpretation of another of Peter's moments of prominence, at the end of the Gospel of John (21.15–17): "Simon son of John, lovest thou me more than these?" . . . "Yea, Lord, thou knowest that I love thee." . . . "Feed my lambs." And again: "Feed my sheep." The usual explanation makes Peter the exemplar both of a particularly fervent love for Christ, and of the special obligation for prelates to exercise the two great precepts of charity, love of God and love of neighbor. The fifteenth-century Denis the Carthusian explains that Christ questioned Peter

> so that He might teach that the prelate over others ought not only to love Christ, but ought also to love Him more fervently than others. . . . As though the Savior said: "In this it will appear that you love Me, if worthily you will feed my servants. . . . Because you love Me, you are fit to feed the flock of my people. . . ."[4]

In finally interpreting Anima's cryptic *Petrus, id est, Christus,* we should remember that it has grown out of Will's question about whether clerks who keep Holy Church know Charity. Seen in this context and in the light of the traditional commentaries I have cited, our passage answers, first, that neither clerks nor others can "know Charity" without the spontaneous, burning love for Christ manifested by Peter the Apostle, typified here in Piers Plowman; and secondly, that by means of such devotion one becomes Piers Plowman—here a figure of Christ through love, as Peter is a figure of Christ both through love and through his prelateship, and as the rock is a figure of Christ through its significance in Scripture.

My final example from *Piers Plowman* is the description of

Christ's leechcraft, in the swift resumé of His life following the Allegory of the Tree. In the B-Text it is Piers who teaches Christ leechcraft—a difficult reference, which has been the despair of one of the keenest scholars to write on the poem in recent years.[5] In what sense can Piers, primarily a symbol of man, be said to teach Christ? Let us approach the passage by way of its clearer counterpart in the C-Text, which substitutes *Liberum-Arbitrium* for Piers:

And in the wombe of that wenche . he was fourty wokes,
And man by-cam of that mayde . to saue mankynde,
Byg and abydynge . and bold in hus barn-hede,
To hauen fouhten with the feende . ar ful tyme come.
Ac *Liberum-Arbitrium* . leche-crafte hym tauhte,
Til *plenitudo temporis* . hih tyme a-prochede,
That suche a surgeyn setthen . yseye was ther neuere,
Ne non so faithfol fysician . for, alle that hym bysouhte,
He lechede hem of here langoure . lazars and blynde bothe;
Ceci uident, claudi ambulant, leprosi mundantur:
And commune wymmen conuertede . and clansede hem of synne. (C-Text XIX.134–43)

We may begin by observing that the central lines (136–41) are obviously an allegory, related to the larger allegory of the Christ-Knight; that they are part of a chronological though drastically condensed telling of the Gospel story; and that they occur between clear references to Christ's birth and to His public life. I believe that these lines allegorize, in highly compressed form, a series of events occupying a corresponding place in the Gospel of Luke, from near the end of Chapter 2 to about the middle of Chapter 4: the child Jesus in the temple; Christ's baptism; His fasting and temptation in the desert; and His reading in the synagogue at Nazareth.

Lines 136–37 of our passage allegorize the verse introducing the story of Jesus in the temple (Luke 2.40): "And the child grew, and was made steadfast full of wisdom; and the grace of God was in Him." Line 136 seems to reflect this verse in detail—"byg" corresponding to "the child grew," defined in commentaries as a reference to physical growth; "abydynge" corresponding to "was made steadfast full of wisdom"; and "bold" corresponding to "the grace of God was in Him." Line 137 alludes to the frequent comment that Christ realized His full powers at the age of twelve, but waited until the *plenitudo temporis* of thirty to begin His public life.

Langland's association of *Liberum-Arbitrium* with the Holy Ghost has been clearly shown by Talbot Donaldson.[6] In Luke and its commentaries, the unifying theme of Christ's baptism, fasting and temptation, and reading in the synagogue is His guidance by the Holy Ghost, Who descends on Him at His baptism, fills Him and leads Him into the desert, and afterwards directs Him back into Galilee (Luke 3.22; 4.1, 14). Lines 138–40 of our passage seem to be a conflated allegory of this theme; their reference to it, however, is by way of the verses from Isaias which Christ reads in the synagogue (Luke 4.18–19), interpreted by commentators as an epitome of His baptism, fasting and temptation, and subsequent miracles:

> The Spirit of the Lord is upon Me, wherefore He hath annointed Me; He hath sent Me to preach the gospel to the poor, to heal the contrite of heart:
>
> To preach deliverance to the captives, and sight to the

blind, to set at liberty them that are bruised, to preach the acceptable year of the Lord, and the day of reward.

Medieval commentary on these verses of Luke provides the images of the Holy Ghost as Christ's teacher; of Christ as physician; and of the fullness of time. The great thirteenth-century commentator Hugh of St. Cher explains in part:

> *The Spirit of the Lord*. . . . In this [verse it is signified that Christ] is less than the Holy Ghost, insofar as He is man. . . . Likewise it is signified that He performed all the exhortations of the Holy Ghost. For He had upon Him the Holy Ghost as counsellor and teacher. . . .
>
> *To heal the contrite of heart*. . . . [that is,] the Lord as the true physician heals [contrite sinners] with repentance. . . . For the words and commands of Christ are medicinal.
>
> *The acceptable year of the Lord,* that is, so that I might show the time of the fullness of grace to have come. . . .[7]

The expression *plenitudo temporis*—used in the New Testament only of the Nativity and the Last Judgment—is frequent in medieval commentary as a reference to the beginning of Christ's public life. After line 141 the allegorical theme of Christ's leechcraft blends into the literal account of His miracles, which in Luke (4.33 ff.) follows His reading in the synagogue.

Let us now turn back to the more difficult passage in the B-Text:

> And in the wombe of that wenche . was he fourty wokes,
> Tyl he wex a faunt thorw her flesshe . and of fiȝtyng couthe,
> To haue y-fouȝte with the fende . ar ful tyme come.

And Pieres the Plowman . parceyued plenere tyme,
And lered hym lechecrafte . his lyf for to saue,
That thowgh he were wounded with his enemye . to warisshe hym-self;
And did him assaye his surgerye . on hem that syke were,
Til he was parfit practisoure . if any peril felle,
And souȝte oute the syke . and synful bothe,
And salued syke and synful . bothe blynde and crokede,
And comune wommen conuerted . and to good torned;
Non est sanis opus medicus, set infirmis, etc.

(XVI. 100–110)

Much of what I have said about the passage in the C-Text will apply here also; the significant difference is in lines 103–6. One additional detail from our chapters in Luke is "to warisshe hym-self," echoing Christ's words, "Physician, heal thyself" (Luke 4.23), a few verses after His reading in the synagogue. Commentary on this verse develops the popular theme of Christ as man's spiritual physician, often in the light of the medieval commonplace that what Christ preached He also performed. Usually it includes a reference to Christ's further remark (Luke 5.31) that the physician is needed not by the healthy but by the sick—a variant of which is quoted in the Latin tag following line 110. Medieval interpretation of this and other related biblical verses presents Christ as the unique physician who by His own wounds healed the sickness of mankind; as both healer, and warrior against the devil; and as the physician who first drinks the bitter medicine of temptation, hardship, and suffering which He prescribes, lest the sick man should hesitate.

Now, within this context of allusion, what are we to make of

Piers Plowman teaching Christ leechcraft? An acceptable interpretation of Piers, I take it, must bear some relation to the pertinent part of the Gospel narrative; must allow Piers to teach Christ without violating his own fundamental role in the poem as man; and must credibly permit the substitution of *Liberum-Arbitrium* for Piers in the C-Text. Though the reference remains a difficult one, I believe these conditions are best met by a complex relationship between Piers and John the Baptist. John's prominence at Christ's baptism is obvious. His perceiving "plenere tyme" would allude generally to the *plenitudo temporis* of the beginning of Christ's public life, mentioned earlier; specifically, it would refer to the *plenitudo temporis* in which John himself began to preach—a familiar idea, developed by commentators from the list of rulers and high priests which in Luke (3.1–2) immediately precedes his preaching. John's relation to what is constant in the Piers-symbol would be through his traditional role as the last and greatest prophet, a representative of what Talbot Donaldson has called "that elevated portion of mankind which includes the patriarchs and prophets—Moses, Abraham, David, Adam, and the others who prefigured Christ before the Incarnation just as St. Peter became Christ's vicar after the Ascension."[8] In terms of the surface Gospel narrative, John's teaching Christ leechcraft might be read as an allegorizing of his visible human role as precursor of Christ (much emphasized in the commentaries), living a similarly blameless life, preparing Christ's way by preaching a similar gospel, and at Christ's baptism serving as minister of the Holy Ghost. The more important allegorical significance of John's teaching Christ, however, would depend on the common spiritual interpretation of

John as God's grace, here obviously suggesting the grace of the Holy Ghost by which Christ is taught after His baptism—and, incidentally, providing an understandable basis for the substitution of *Liberum-Arbitrium* (the Holy Ghost) in the C-Text. Hugh of St. Cher's comment on the later episode in which John sends his disciples to question Christ (Luke 7.19–22) establishes a meaningful connection between this spiritual interpretation of John and the theme of Christ's leechcraft:

> Mystically, John the Baptist is baptismal grace. . . . Note, moreover, what [Christ] says: "Report to John," that is, to the grace of God, to which the preacher ought to attribute whatever of good he performs or speaks. . . . In the following [verses], note what the preaching of Christ performs.[9]

The account of Christ's "preaching" which follows is really a spiritual interpretation of His leechcraft, based on the biblical verse (Luke 7.22) inserted near the end of our C-Text passage: *Ceci vident, claudi ambulant, leprosi mundantur.* Finally, to this whole proposed interpretation of Piers one should add that it would not necessarily rule out an interpretation of him in terms of Christ's own human psychology, if a convincing one can ever be found; and that in any case, here as elsewhere in the poem, Piers as idealized mankind suggests Christ implicitly—a suggestion actually strengthened by the allusion to John, himself traditionally a figure of Christ.

Examples from *Piers Plowman* could be multiplied almost indefinitely, had we but Weltanschauung enough and time. But if these few have carried the conviction I hope they have, you may be waiting to hear what sort of exegetical allusion I will claim for Chaucer. I assume that no one will deny him a certain limited use of fairly obvious images, like for example those in the *Prioress' Prologue* and *Tale;* but his more interesting uses of exegetical imagery are generally less obvious. Let us begin with a small but distinct example.

Among the unsavory details that go to make up Chaucer's portrait of the Summoner is the line in the *General Prologue,*

> Wel loved he garleek, oynons, and eek lekes. (l. 634)

The garlic, onions, and leeks have been convincingly explained by W. C. Curry as notorious irritants of the Summoner's leprosy. In addition, however, it is possible to see in them an exegetical allusion paralleling the general drift of Professor Curry's interpretation, based on the murmuring of the Hebrew people in Numbers 11.5, "We remember the fish that we ate in Egypt, gratis. The cucumbers and melons come into our mind, and the leeks and onions and garlic."

Medieval commentary furnishes pertinent associations. The often-repeated comment of Gregory, for example, suggests a spiritual parallel to the Summoner's dietary perversity in loving the very foods that aggravate his discomfort:

> Through the leeks and onions, whose eaters commonly shed tears, what is expressed but the distresses of the present life, which also is pursued not without sorrow by those who love it, though it is loved with tears? Leaving the manna therefore, they seek after . . . the leeks and onions, because indeed evil souls despise gifts sweet with the charm of quiet, and for the sake of carnal delights they desire the toilsome

> paths of this life, even though full of tears; they disdain to have that by which they might spiritually rejoice, and eagerly strive after that by which they may carnally groan.

Similar interpretations are found in many later commentaries and other exegetical works—among them Peter Riga's *Aurora,* cited by Chaucer as the source for a detail in the *Book of the Duchess* (l. 1169). Most interesting of all is the entry in an anonymous *Liber de Moralitatibus* preserved in several manuscript copies,[10] which not only interprets spiritually the physical connection between garlic and some of the symptoms of leprosy, but includes other interpretations suggesting the Summoner's general spiritual depravity, his corrupting influence on others (ll. 649–51, 653–58, 663–65), his own lustfulness (ll. 626, 652), and his blindness to realities beyond the material (ll. 653–58):

> Garlic [*allium*] has these conditions or properties. First, as Isidore says, it is so named from *olendo,* because it smells. This signifies one stinking with vicious practices. . . . Third, as [Dioscorides] says, it upsets and greatly dries up the stomach and the digestion. This signifies the vice of avarice, which disturbs and saddens the family possessing it. . . . Fourth, as he also says, when applied to the body it ulcerates and wounds. This signifies that bad men corrupt those who are intimate with them. . . . Fifth, as he also says, if it is much in use it inflames the body, generates leprosy, excites mania and frenzy, injures and weakens the sight, and therefore is harmful to those choleric by nature; for it quickly generates red choler, and multiplies and augments adust. This signifies that in a spiritual way, worldly love performs

> all these same evils in the soul. . . . Twelfth, as he also says, if it is eaten continually or too much, it is harmful to the vision. This signifies that the lustfulness or wantonness which exists in wicked habit prevents all awareness of things heavenly. . . .

Similar interpretations are found in the great fourteenth-century *Reductorium* of Bersuire.

I propose, then, that Chaucer is using this detail in the portrait of the Summoner with its exegetical overtones as well as its medical ones, to deepen an already ugly picture of spiritual as well as physical deformity. Possibly the exegetical echo is to be seen as the comment of Chaucer the author, playing over the more factual medical observation of Chaucer the character in his own poem. At any rate, the allusion has at least one colorful precedent. Liutprand of Cremona, writing in the tenth century to deplore the rulership, mores, and person of the Byzantine emperor Nicephorus Phocas, concludes a catalogue of uncharitable allusion with the picture of Nicephorus "stuffing himself with garlic, onion, and leeks, drinking bathwater." Liutprand proceeds to a pious contrast of the habit with that of his own lord, Otto I, "*not* stuffing himself with garlic, onions, and leeks so that by this means he may spare the animals. . . ." East is East and West is West, but one detects biblical innuendo at the expense of historical fact—especially since Liutprand's added insult about sparing the animals seems to reflect a commentary on the preceding verse of Numbers (11.4), according to which the Hebrews asked God for meat while sparing their own animals out of avarice. The four centuries and half a continent which separate Chaucer from Liutprand serve, if anything, to highlight the evidence; with all their differences, the Vulgate plus commentary would have been one of the obvious traditions open to them both.

It seems to me that these several factors taken together must carry a degree of conviction difficult to escape. And in this instance, the biblical allusion itself would surely be pointless without reference to the exegetical tradition behind it. If one accepts this reading of what has so far appeared to be a quite literal surface detail, the implication seems to be that Chaucer was capable of using exegetical allusion in ways hitherto little recognized, and that we will be wise to explore his work further in this direction. Especially provocative examples are the theme of the Scriptural eunuch and the Pauline "Old Man" in the *Pardoner's Tale,* analyzed by Robert P. Miller;[11] and the echoes from the Canticle of Canticles in the *Merchant's Tale* and the *Miller's Tale.* Robertson has offered what seems to me a correct interpretation of these echoes in the *Merchant's Tale* (ll. 2138–48).[12] In the *Miller's Tale,* the allusions to Canticles are organized around a broadly comic association of Absolon with the bridegroom and of Alisoun with the bride. Let us first recapture the major echoes themselves, beginning with the most obvious.

Absolon's fateful second arrival beneath Alisoun's window is self-heralded by a baroque plea, stylistically rather unlike anything else in the tale:

> "What do ye, hony-comb, sweete Alisoun,
> My faire bryd, my sweete cynamome?
> Awaketh, lemman myn, and speketh to me!
> Wel litel thynken ye upon my wo,

That for youre love I swete ther I go.
No wonder is thogh that I swelte and swete;
I moorne as dooth a lamb after the tete.
Ywis, lemman, I have swich love-longynge,
That lik a turtel trewe is my moornynge.
I may nat ete na moore than a mayde." (ll. 3696–3707)

The situation here, with the lover pleading outside the chamber of his beloved, parallels generally that in the second and fifth chapters of Canticles; more important, however, are a number of detailed correspondences between Absolon's plea itself and these same two general parts of Canticles. His first two lines, for example, contain three echoes from near the end of Chapter 4:

Thy lips, *my bride,* [are] as a dropping *honeycomb;*
honey and milk [are] under thy tongue. . . .
Spikenard and saffron, sweet cane and *cinnamon,*
with all the trees of Libanus. . . . (Cant. 4.11, 14)

While Absolon's ambiguous "my faire bryd" (able to mean either a bride, woman, or bird) is in itself no novelty in Middle English love poetry, I know of no comparable and straightforward uses of "hony-comb" or "cynamome"; the latter seems pointedly to echo the *cinnamomum* of the Vulgate, since the much more usual word for cinnamon in Middle English is "canel." Absolon's third line,

Awaketh, lemman myn, and speketh to me!

is a paraphrase of Canticles 2.13, 14—

Awake, my love . . .
let thy voice sound in my ears. . . .

Having established his reference to Canticles by concentrating four recognizable echoes into these first three lines, Chaucer proceeds to fill the rest of Absolon's plea with comic variations on the theme. Time will not permit a detailed exposition; but by way of example, we may notice the bridegroom's beautiful love-plaint—

> . . . my head is full of dew,
> and my locks [are full of] the drops of the nights
> (5.2)

—which degenerates soggily into

> That for youre love I swete ther I go.

Again, in this frame of reference Absolon's "love-longynge" suggests the famous *Quia amore langueo* of Canticles 2.5 and 5.8; while his reference to the mourning turtle, besides its non-biblical associations, can recall the voice of the turtle in Canticles 2.12—interpreted in medieval commentary as the mourning of the devout soul over the slowness of earthly life, which keeps it from its heavenly reward.

These echoes in Absolon's plea inevitably color the events which follow. One is led to think, for example, of the sensuous dignity of the bride's response in Canticles:

> I arose that I might open to my beloved;
> my hands dropped myrrh,
> and my fingers [were] full of the choicest myrrh.
> (5.5)

Alisoun's reply gains in economy what it loses in elegance:

> "Go fro the wyndow, Jakke fool," she sayde. (l. 3708)

Or there is the stately and repeated request in Canticles, interpreted by commentators as loving solicitude on the part of the bridegroom—

> I adjure you, daughters of Jerusalem,
> by the roes and harts of the fields,
> that you stir not up, nor make [my] beloved to waken,
> until she please. (Cant. 2.7; 3.5; 8.4)

—and against it, Alisoun's self-solicitous yell:

> Go forth thy wey, or I wol caste a ston,
> And lat me slepe, a twenty devel wey! (l. 3712–13)

Once aware of these echoes in and around Absolon's plea, we may find ourselves taking a fresh look also at Chaucer's introductory portraits of Alisoun and Absolon. The first long *effictio* of Alisoun includes the lines,

> Hir mouth was sweete as bragot or the meeth,
> Or hoord of apples leyd in hey or heeth. (3261–62)

These two details clearly echo a description of the bride in Canticles:

> . . . the odor of thy mouth [is] like apples.
> Thy throat [is] like the best wine. . . . (7.8–9)

In addition, the pictures of the two women are full of tantalizing half-correspondences, which cumulatively suggest a naturalistic reworking of the exotic imagery of Canticles by Chaucer. At the risk one always runs by quoting such parallels in isolation, I call your attention to Alisoun's brooch as broad as the boss of a buckler (ll. 3265–66) and the "thousand bucklers" that make up the necklace of the bride in Canticles 4.4—two rather unusual figures, used in approximately corresponding parts of the two portraits. Or there is the description of Alisoun's frisking—

> Therto she koude skippe and make game. . . .
> Wynsynge she was. . . .
> Hir shoes were laced on hir legges hye
> (ll. 3259, 3263, 3267)

—and the famous Canticles 7.1:

> How beautiful are thy steps in shoes, O prince's daughter!

A little later in the tale, Absolon is described:

> Crul was his heer, and as the gold it shoon,
> And strouted as a fanne large and brode;
> Ful streight and evene lay his joly shode.
> His rode was reed, his eyen greye as goos.
> (ll. 3314–17)

In Canticles, our basic reference in chapters 4 and 5 is followed at no great distance by a description of the bridegroom:

> My beloved [is] white and ruddy,
> chosen out of thousands.
> His head [is as] the finest gold.
> His locks [are] as the upright branches of palm trees. . . .
> His eyes [are] as doves upon brooks of waters. . . .
> (5.10–12)

Though Absolon's golden hair and fresh complexion clearly have their origin in a medieval *effictio* of the biblical Absalom, I am not sure that this disqualifies them as echoes also of the bridegroom's golden head and of his white and ruddy complexion. The essential picture in the bridegroom's hair like standing palm-fronds is caught, but comically, by Absolon's hair that "strouted as a fanne large and brode." The dove in this passage, according to medieval commentators, signifies wisdom; the goose who is substituted in the description of Absolon seems clearly to suggest folly, a significance she bears consistently in Chaucer as elsewhere. Finally, the description of the bridegroom in Canticles continues:

His cheeks [are] as beds of aromatic spices,
set by the perfumers.
His lips [are] lilies,
dropping choice myrrh. . . .
His throat [is] most sweet,
and [he is] wholly desirable. . . . (5.13, 16)

One recalls Absolon's preparations a few lines before his plea:

But first he cheweth greyn and lycorys,
To smellen sweete, er he hadde kembd his heer.
Under his tonge a trewe-love he beer,
For therby wende he to ben gracious. (ll. 3690–93)

Several further correspondences can be found, including a probable outrageous connection between Absolon's kiss and the famous opening verse of Canticles. Whether one accepts all of my proposed examples or not, I suppose that any serious disagreement about this series of echoes would center not so much on its existence as on its degree of meaningfulness. Without invoking complex external arguments from the nature of medieval thought and poetic expression, it seems to me that within the tale itself everything is against our reading these parallels as superficial verbal borrowings. First, there is the pattern of increasing elaborateness and perceptibility into which they fall: the single distinct allusion and the probable surrounding hints in the description of Alisoun; the more concentrated echoes in the description of Absolon; and finally the full expansion of the parodic theme in the situation and the series of allusions in and around Absolon's plea. Second, there are the other obvious strains of biblical allusion in the *Miller's Tale*—one embracing Absolon's name and his biblical hair, medieval exegeses of which have been conveniently assembled by Father Beichner; [13] and another the pervasive theme of Noe and the Deluge. And third, there is the indicative fact that Chaucer has seen fit to attach echoes of Canticles to precisely two such futile lovers as Absolon and January.

So far, I have said almost nothing about medieval commentary on Canticles. Its controlling ideas can be stated briefly: the bridegroom signifies Christ; his bride is the Church or the individual Christian soul; the love of the bridegroom for the bride, and the sexual love to which he exhorts her, is the spiritual perfection of charity. To whatever extent our pattern of allusions may be admitted in the *Miller's Tale,* their common significances seem to me fairly clear. On the simplest level of comedy there is the very incongruity of Canticles and its mystical associations set into the fabliau context, plus the inversions and other comic variations performed on individual verses. Only slightly more complex is the picture of the foolish and effeminate Absolon, his fate as a lover, and his ungallant concept of revenge, beside the elevated and successful love of the bridegroom; and along with it the shrill vulgarity of Alisoun—a side of her that comes out only in her dealings with Absolon, and consistently there—beside the gracious compliance of the bride. Underlying the whole series of allusions, however, is a more important contrast between the carnality of Absolon and Alisoun, and the charity of bridegroom and bride. As divine charity is fitly portrayed through the exalted imagery of Canticles, so carnal cupidity is not only dramatically presented but in part also figuratively defined in the hopeless folly of Absolon, the sluttish action and speech of Alisoun, and the inexorable obscenity of the carnal lover's reward.

For the attachment of this biblical and exegetical theme to a character obviously suggesting the biblical Absalom, there is an immediate basis in the medieval identification of the author and literal bridegroom of Canticles as Solomon, together with the natural parallel between Solomon and Absalom as sons of David and their traditional contrasts in other respects. Medieval interpretations of Absalom consistently oppose him to precisely the perfections of the bridegroom—either identifying him with various arch-enemies of Christ or associating him with the negation or perversion of charity, very often by way of carnal desire. Through such channels he sometimes finds his way into the commentaries on Canticles itself. In the *Miller's Tale,* the whole comic association between Absolon and the divine bridegroom seems subtly reinforced shortly after Absolon's plea, by a pair of juxtapositions which for simple expletive have always struck me as rather oddly fashioned:

> "I love another—and elles I were to blame—
> Wel bet than thee, *by Jhesu, Absolon.*"

. . . . .

> "Thanne kysse me, syn it may be no bet,
> *For Jhesus love, and for the love of me.*"
>
> (ll. 3710–11, 3716–17)

At the beginning of this paper I made basically two assertions. One was that the most convincing argument for the importance of exegetical interpretation lies in specific, documented examples of its importance. By these intervening examples, I have tried to show that the exegetical tradition is used with artistic intent by Langland and Chaucer; and that its controlled application to medieval literature constitutes a valuable though difficult aid to literary interpretation.[14] To this statement I should add that so far as one can tell, work of this kind is still close to its beginning. Its canons, methods, and major sources are still relatively undefined; some of what should be its basic apparatus is antiquated or nonexistent; and the great bulk of thirteenth- and fourteenth-century commentaries remain unprinted. My other beginning assertion was that exegetical imagery and allusion are employed by medieval writers with a poetic variety and subtlety much greater than is sometimes supposed. I hope that this claim too has found support, in the variety of meanings and emotional effects toward which we have seen exegetical images used—ranging from the sublimity of Book's apocalyptic time-vision to the civilized moral comedy of Chaucer.

SUMMATION

Charles Donahue

THE REAL AREA of difference on patristic exegesis has now been pointed out. Mr. Kaske has shown clearly how the use of material from the exegetical tradition can clarify individual points in difficult texts and suggest new dimensions of meaning in texts already understood. Mr. Donaldson, however, conceded in advance that such possibilities exist. What disturbed him were the apparent lapses from accepted philological method into which the search for the spiritual meaning sometimes leads modern commentators who belong to what I am going to call, because I need a name, the "pan-allegorical school." These lapses seem to be caused, perhaps justified, by two basic assumptions of the school:

1. Patristic and medieval exegetes cared little for the letter, the text, and were interested mainly in higher spiritual meanings reached by allegory.

2. The exegetical conviction that "the letter killeth but the spirit quickeneth" had a profound influence on all, or almost all, medieval poets. A corollary of this assumption is the further as-

sumption that all, or almost all, medieval poems are to be approached as allegories.

The task of the modern expositor is to find the hidden meaning. If the uncovering of the hidden meaning results in considerable neglect of details in the literal text—Mr. Donaldson illustrated how this could happen—the modern critic need not be disturbed. The medieval writer was not interested in the husk of the letter but in the nourishing corn, the allegorical meaning.

Of the two problems relevant to the area of difference, the problem of the nature of patristic and medieval exegesis and the problem of the effect of that tradition on the imagination and methods of medieval poets, the first is logically prior to the second. It has, however, received relatively little attention. My purpose is to put this first problem forward as a subject for investigation. Obviously, I hope to settle nothing in the course of a brief paper, but it may be possible to determine within the exegetical tradition some *points d'appui* from which sorties may later be made and ground cleared.

Perhaps we can best commence our examination of a tradition consisting of Hebraic intertwined with Hellenic elements by thinking for a moment of Erich Auerbach's suggestive contrast between the narrative method of Homer and that of the historical books of the Old Testament. Homer presents fixed states. Achilles, the young warrior; Odysseus, the mature man of action who seems to change little in the course of his adventures; Nestor, the old sage: these are types who "appear to be of an age fixed from the very first." In sharp contrast, the Old Testament is interested in process and person, in the road, for example, that lay between "David, the harp player, persecuted by his lord's jealousy, and the old king, surrounded by violent intrigues, whom Abishag the Shunnamite warmed in his bed and he knew her not!"[1] In short, the earliest documents, as Auerbach sees them, adumbrate on the one hand the Hebraic concern with the complexities of concrete reality and, on the other, the Greek tendency to move by way of abstraction from the concrete real to a world of clear and manageable ideas.

Both tendencies affected Christian exegesis. The first influence was Hebraic. Let us look a little more closely at it. The Hebrew lived in a created universe. The work of the Most High, eminently intelligible in itself, is full of mysteries for any creature, even such a creature as man, created in "the image and likeness of God" and capable of a kind of humble familiarity with Him. Hence, the Hebraic interest in process. David, for example, is God's creature, and his existence must be significant. But, since this significance works itself out in time, no creature can grasp it at any one point in the process. In David's end is his beginning. What is true of individual lives is true of the lives of nations. The national life of the People of the Covenant, particularly, is meaningful as part of the divine plan; but that meaning, in its fullness, cannot be grasped by man who must await its revelation in the "fullness of time." The late prophets are clearly looking forward to a messianic era where the full meaning of the words and deeds recorded in the holy writings will be revealed.

Christianity was born in an atmosphere of Jewish messianic expectation. The earliest Christian exegesis is thoroughly Judaic in spirit. Clearly, the evangelists regard the life and words of the Lord as a living interpretation revealing in history the full meaning of the holy writings. To take one example: In the

Twenty-first Psalm, David, calling out, "My God, why hast thou forsaken me," speaks of his sense of abandonment by God, of his sufferings, and of his hope that God will rescue him and enable him to proclaim God's name among all his brethren. The psalm may have been originally an expression of David's personal experience. It was read in the Temple and synagogues and doubtless acquired other meanings for those who used it. The plenitude of its meaning, however, appears only in the fullness of time when it is recited by the Lord on the cross (Matt. 27.46).

The Epistle to the Hebrews (7.1–28) discusses the priesthood of Christ and contrasts it with the Levitical priesthood by establishing a parallel between the gentile Melchisedech, king of Salem, and Christ. Melchisedech, priest of the Most High, brought out bread and wine and blessed Abraham (Gen. 14.18–20). The meaning of the concrete person Melchisedech and of his bread and wine becomes clear only in time through Christ and the institution of the eucharist.

Early exegesis outside the canonical books worked in the same Hebraic spirit. In a fragment believed to be by Melito of Sardis (fl. 161–80), Abraham's offering of Isaac is viewed as a prefiguration of the death of Christ.[2] These examples illustrate the earlier method of exegesis. Essentially, that method consists in establishing a parallel between two concrete things: persons, as in the case of Melchisedech and Christ; events, as in the sacrifice of Isaac and the crucifixion; or utterances, as those of David in Psalm 21 and of Christ on the cross. From the parallel springs an insight into the mysterious providence of God working through events, persons, utterances. The method is historical, concrete, Hebraic. The word "allegory" as that word is commonly understood does not describe it. To distinguish it from allegorical interpretation, the earlier and Hebraic method is now sometimes called "typological." [3]

Allegory, as we understand it, does enter the tradition, but it comes in from quite a different source. The Greek interest in the static and the general, noticed already in Homer by Auerbach, led naturally to that concern for universal truth and that suspicion of what seemed the shadow-show of concrete reality which is reflected in Plato's allegory of the cave. At least a century before Plato, philosophical objection had been made to the conduct of Homer's gods. Greeks who felt the charm of Homer's poetry and who were perhaps moved by *pietas* towards a body of writings incorporating traditional wisdom attempted to reply by maintaining that Homer's gods were not gods nor were they intended to be. They were merely poetical devices for talking about natural or psychic forces. This suggestion seems to have been made as early as the late sixth century B.C. By the third century, the Stoic Cleanthes of Assos was using the now familiar word. He speaks of interpreting *allēgorikōs*. The method was favored by those concerned to reconcile philosophical convictions with the rather unphilosophical things one often finds in poetry. It was applied to Homer by Stoics such as Crates (3d cent. B.C.), by neo-Platonists such as Porphyry, and later, in the Byzantine period, by Christians such as Tzetzes (d. 1180).[4] In the West, Virgil was interpreted allegorically by Macrobius and Fulgentius (*ca.*500), and the method was, apparently, widely used in interpreting classical authors in the medieval schools.[5]

It is apparent that Greek allegorizing is basically different from the early Christian typological approach to exegesis. Typology finds a hitherto unsuspected layer of meaning in the original record, but the person, event, or utterance of the record retains all its original existence and value. Melchisedech is no less Melchisedech when he has been discovered to be a *tupos* of Christ. In the Greek method, the original meaning is destroyed once the allegorical meaning has been discovered. The Athene who pulled Achilles by the hair evaporates into a *bella menzogna* if we say that the passage really means that Achilles's prudence restrained his wrath. The grain has been winnowed out, and what is left is only more or less picturesque chaff.

Nevertheless, Greek allegorizing did become a part of the Christian exegetical tradition. Reared in the pluralistic society of Alexandria, Philo adapted the methods of Greek interpretation to the Hebrew Scriptures.[6] Alexandrine Christians, some of whom had come to Christianity by way of Plato, followed his example. Greek allegorizing plays a part in the exegetical work of Origen.[7] Despite objections from more conservative exegetes, he appealed to those Christians who would have agreed with Augustine in regarding Plato as the philosopher closest to Christianity.

Origen's methods became known in the West and indubitably affected the three great Western Fathers, Ambrose, Jerome, and Augustine. Ambrose was directly acquainted with the work of Philo, and, like Origen, he uses both typology and allegory in the Greek sense. They are not distinguished. Both are regarded as means of attaining meanings higher than the literal meaning, the *sensus altior* or *subtilior interpretatio*.[8] Ambrose, let us remember, was primarily a Christian pastor, a preacher, and a guide of souls. Most of his exegetical work is apparently compiled from his homilies. The advantages of Greek allegory for the homilist are obvious. It gives him an opportunity to draw useful moral lessons from passages in scripture where the moral lesson in the literal meaning is by no means obvious. It also provides him with means of skirting certain Old Testament passages where the literal sense, as for example in the references to polygamy in the Old Testament, might be puzzling to the simpler numbers of his flock. Greek allegory, in short, was particularly useful in drawing what came to be called the moral or tropological sense. Even here, however, one can observe in Ambrose a considerable modification of the Greek method. In Greek allegorical interpretation, the literal text becomes a *bella menzogna*. Even when he draws allegorical morals from it, Ambrose never questions the importance or the veracity of the literal text.[9] Like Ambrose, Jerome started as an admirer of Origen. He moved away from allegory, however, to a more purely philological interest in the literal text.

Ambrose was an important influence in the conversion of Augustine, who was impressed by Ambrose's allegorical homilies on scripture.[10] Augustine's first important exegetical work, the *De Genesi contra Manichaeos,* is written in the Ambrosian manner. About five years later, Augustine turned to Genesis again, and this time he attempted to expound the literal text. With a keen sense of the difficulties involved, he abandoned the work, the *De Genesi ad Litteram, Liber Imperfectus*. Again in 401 he set himself to the same task and worked at it intermittently for fourteen years. The result, the *De Genesi ad Litteram Libri Duodecem,* was still unsatisfactory.[11] "More questions than answers will be found there," he writes in the *Retractationes* (XXIV), "and of the answers few are solidly based; the others are only proposed to suggest new questions." [12] Obviously, Augustine was no scorner of the letter. His appreciation of the difficulties of literal interpretation and of the value of the textual and linguistic approach of his contemporary Jerome grew with his years and experience as an exegete.

Of the three Western Fathers, Augustine made the most substantial contribution to doctrinal development. It is, I believe, worth noting that in the controversial works where, for example, the doctrine of grace is established against the Pelagians, no appeal is made to allegorical interpretation. Augustine bases doctrine on the letter of scripture, taken, of course, in context. Of Augustine's more speculative, as opposed to his doctrinal, works, the most noteworthy is the *City of God*. Here, he uses "mystical" interpretation, but this interpretation is more often typological, Hebraic, than allegorical in the Greek sense. Indeed, the entire work is the classic exposition of the Hebraic sense of the meaningfulness of the concrete historical event. Augustine's use of Greek, or rather Ambrosian, allegory is most frequent in works such as the *Enarrationes in Psalmos* which are homiletic in character.[13]

Augustine's manual on how to read the Bible, the *De Doctrina Christiana,* a work frequently appealed to by modern allegorical critics, is addressed to the cultivated Christian who wishes to make a serious study of scripture. Augustine has in mind primarily future clerics who will preach. The last book is given over to the art of preaching. But the *De Doctrina* is also a work intended for anyone who wants to make scripture a basis for private meditation. It is not a manual on the use of scripture for doctrinal development, for theologians in our sense of the word.

The first necessity for a fruitful reading of scripture, according to Augustine, is an acquaintance with Christian dogma and moral doctrine. These are set forth in the first book. Armed with a doctrine derived from ecclesiastical tradition and based on unambiguous scriptural texts, the student may approach scripture safely if he will remember the first rule for scriptural interpretation, which is that the end and fulfillment of the law and of all the holy writings is love of God and neighbor. He who thinks he understands scripture deceives himself unless his understanding builds in him this twin charity. Indeed, anyone who derives a meaning from scripture useful for forming charity has not gone dangerously astray even if that meaning can be shown to be different from that intended by the inspired author. (There is, to be sure, some danger in all error, and the student should be corrected if possible. But the matter is not serious.[14]) Here, Augustine seems to have in mind the private Christian of only moderate learning who takes up the study of scripture mainly for personal edification.

In the second book Augustine is apparently thinking of readers with wider opportunities for study, perhaps future clerics and preachers. He is very emphatic on the necessity of sound philological equipment for such students. They should take pains to get the best texts available. They should compare various translations. They must know Greek, and they can use as much Hebrew as they can get.[15] Since *things* as well as words are significant in scripture, students ought also to bring an extensive knowledge of things to bear on their exegetical problems. They should have made a systematic study of human things, such as dialectic, the laws of human reasoning. They should be broadly read in human history. Knowledge of nonhuman things derived from mathematics and what we would call science is also valuable.

The service of Augustine's program in keeping alive in the Iron Age which followed his death the ideal of a reasonably broad and humane education has often been noticed. Not heretofore noticed has been the misuse made by some of the divines of that Iron Age of one paragraph about figurative interpretation in the third book. The third book points out dangers and pitfalls in the study of scripture and gives suggestions as to how to avoid them. One danger is that passages which should be taken figuratively will be taken literally. In this connection Augustine cites II Corinthians 3.6—*Littera occidit, spiritus autem vivificat*—and then goes on thus: "When one takes properly what is said figuratively, one learns carnally. Nor can anything be more rightly called a death of the mind than when the intelligence, by which the mind excels the brutes, is subjected to the flesh in following the letter. He who follows the letter takes figurative words in a non-figurative sense and does not find in the thing signified by the word a further meaning. When he hears the word 'sacrifice', for example, his thought does not go beyond the sacrifice of beasts and fruits of the earth which was offered of old. It is indeed a miserable servitude of the mind to take signs for things and to be unable to raise the mind's eye above corporeal creation to draw in the eternal light." [16]

Out of its context, this paragraph invites misunderstanding. We shall see that the invitation was accepted. Augustine certainly does not mean that the letter of scripture, in all cases, is carnal—I suspect he would have regarded such an idea as blasphemous—or that, as a general rule, a figurative interpretation is to be regarded as holier, more "spiritual," than a nonfigurative one. Shortly after the passage quoted, Augustine adds, "To the observation that we should beware of taking a figurative passage literally, a further caution should be added: we should not understand figuratively passages which ought to be understood literally." [17]

The crucial passage from II Corinthians is commented upon also in the *De Spiritu et Littera.* This is a doctrinal work; Augustine's language is more formal and circumspect, and his interpretation of the passage is quite clear. Augustine here says plainly that when the apostle wrote that "the letter killeth but the spirit quickeneth" he did not have in mind figurative as opposed to literal interpretation of scripture. His words, however, may be fittingly applied to that question.[18] A careful examination of the passage from the *De Doctrina,* in its context, shows how Augustine applied them. He clearly has in mind the ritualistic prescriptions of the Old Law. The example he uses is that of the sacrifices of the Old Law. After the passage quoted, he goes on to discuss the spiritual state of the Jews under the Old Law. There are certain things in the Old Testament, Augustine is saying, such as the ritualistic prescriptions of the Mosaic Law, which need not, indeed should not, be taken literally by a Christian. It does not follow, however, that the Christian exegete can ignore these passages. Whatever is written is written for our doctrine. The prescriptions of the Old Law foreshadow the New Law, as, for example, the sacrifices of the Old Law foreshadow the Sacrifice of the New Law.[19] It should be noted that in this passage Augustine is using "Hebraic" historical interpretation, typology, not allegory in the Greek sense.

Augustine is our first important *point d'appui.* He is difficult because his language is that of a literary man, often that of a rhetorician, and lacks the scholastic exactness of that of the later medieval theologians. Nonetheless, I suggest that a careful examination of his work would reveal that the main bent of his exegesis is "Hebraic," typological, rather than allegorical in the Greek sense. If my conjecture is correct, it means that certain divines of the early Middle Ages who apparently believed that Augustine taught that the literal sense is unimportant and a figurative sense always to be preferred were in error, and that the modern critic who looks at Augustine through the eyes of the early medieval divines is in danger of mistaking the basic tendencies of patristic exegesis and of the sounder and more central medieval exegesis.

Augustine died when the barbarians were at the gates of Hippo. During the centuries that followed the disorders occasioned by the invasions imposed upon the Church the task of building a new civilization upon the ruins of Rome. Such a task necessarily changed the character of ecclesiastical activity. It brought to the fore the man of action, the missionary, the preacher, the effective pastor who could mollify somewhat the barbarous manners of his charges. At the same time, the general disorder made the monastery imperative as a center for quiet piety and learning. Figurative interpretation of scripture was useful to the preacher, as we have seen. It was useful also for the meditation of monks. Writing to Acca on the allegorical interpretation of the first book of Samuel, the Venerable Bede exclaims: "If we take care to bring forth from scripture only the deeds of old, that is, follow only the meaning of the letter in the Jewish manner, what correction for our daily sins, what consolation for the swelling cares of the age, what spiritual doctrine do we acquire when, opening the book, for example, of blessed Samuel, we find that one man, Elcana, had two wives—we especially to whom the custom of ecclesiastical life proposes that we abstain from the embrace of woman and remain celibate? What indeed, unless we know how to strike out an allegorical sense from passages of this sort, which will bring lively interior renewal by correcting, teaching, consoling."[20]

In his well known preface to *Genesis,* a document coming from near the end of the period I am calling the Iron Age, Ælfric explains the value of figurative interpretation to the practical pastor as well as for personal meditation. He hesitated, he says, to translate *Genesis* for fear lest "some foolish man who reads the book or hears it read will think he may now live under the New Law as the patriarchs lived in the time before the Old Law had been promulgated or as men lived under the law of Moses." He tells how troubled he was when an old priest who had been his teacher and knew some Latin told him that the Patriarch Jacob had four wives. Such unlearned priests, he says, "if they understand a little Latin immediately think they may be famous teachers, but they do not know the spiritual interpretation and how the old law was a shadowing forth of things to come, and how the new revelation after Christ's incarnation was a fulfilment of all the things which the old revelation foreshadowed concerning Christ and His chosen."[21]

We may note in passing Ælfric's very historical understanding of the term "spiritual interpretation." Our immediate concern with both passages, however, that of Bede and that of Ælfric, is the evidence they afford of the wholly practical exigencies which often determined the character of scriptural exegesis during the Iron Age: problems connected with the development of a monastic spirituality, pastoral problems arising from the low cultural level of many of the clergy and the still lower level of the laity. Add to this the poverty of philological equipment which restricted the activity of even the most learned of the period, such as Bede, and the neglect of dialectic with the precision of expression that art fosters, and one is in a position to evaluate the numerous statements emanating from the divines of the Iron Age which relate the literal to the figurative interpretation of scripture as chaff to grain, kernel to nut, letter which killeth to spirit which quickeneth.[22] These are rhetorical statements by men trained in rhetoric rather than in dialectic. They reflect the concern of the monastic teacher who must find something edifying to say about Elcana and his two wives, or of the pastor who must persuade the local *ealdorman* that he cannot be a good churchman if he conducts his connubial life in the manner of Jacob *secundum litteram*. Some of the statements, particularly those which make use of II Corinthians 3.6, echo the words of Augustine, but they can be regarded, at the most, as only crude approximations to Augustine's subtle and nuanced thought. Even less can they be regarded as reflections of the doctrine of the Church.

It can even be suggested that the divines of the Iron Age failed, in the main, to explicate the deeper instincts towards scripture current in their own period. These instincts, not clearly described in speculative works, find expression in the liturgy. Here, in the monasteries, the Iron Age made a permanent contribution to the life of the Church by erecting the superstructure of the Latin liturgies on the foundations laid in the patristic period. One might almost say that the basic structural principle of these liturgies lies in a parallelism between the Old and the New Testaments, the drawing of significance from one concrete historical reality by relating it to another. This is the same principle we have seen working in the "Hebraic" or typological method of scriptural exegesis. Allegory in the Greek sense plays a very restricted role in the liturgy. For the period from the sixth century to the twelfth our most important *point d'appui* for an investigation of attitudes towards the meaning of scripture may well prove to be the body of liturgical texts.

The twelfth century was, of course, a crucial period in the development of Western religious thought. Here the older, more poetical and intuitive approaches, now grown more articulate, meet the more discursive and dialectical method which is to characterize the scholastic period. The meeting is dramatically symbolized in the opposition between St. Bernard and Abelard. Bernard, however, had far too original a genius to serve as a typical spokesman for any point of view. The writer who best analyzes and presents the profounder tendencies of the previous age—the poetic and symbolic age—is perhaps Hugh of St. Victor. Hugh's basic approach to exegesis is essentially that of Augustine methodized for the use of the teacher. There are three possible readings of scripture, the historical, the allegorical, and the tropological. Hugh is very insistent on the fundamental character of the historical reading. "Fundamentum autem et principium doctrinae sacrae historia est, de qua, quasi mel de favo, veritas allegoriae exprimitur." [23] What Hugh calls allegory arises from a relation between two concrete things: "Allegoria est cum id quod ex littera significatum proponitur aliud sive in praesenti sive in futuro *factum* significatur." [24] Hugh has in mind *inter alia* the "spiritual" interpretation of the ritualistic prescriptions of the Old Law. He mentions Leviticus, Numbers, and Deuteronomy among the books particularly suitable for the allegorical approach. After scripture has been studied first historically, then allegorically, the student is ready to draw moral lessons in a third reading. This is tropological.

Besides the three readings of scripture, Hugh makes use of another methodological triad, the three steps necessarily involved in the exposition of any text, sacred or profane. These three are the *littera,* and *sensus,* and the *sententia.* Hugh tells us very precisely what he means: "The *littera* is the fitting arrangement of verbal material which is also called construction. The *sensus* is the clear and obvious (*aperta*) meaning which the *littera* immediately produces." [25] *Littera* and *sensus* are, then, simply obverse and reverse of the same coin, the grammatical form and its meaning. "The *sententia* is a deeper insight (*profundior intelligentia*) which cannot be found except by exposition and interpretation." I cannot see that by *sententia* Hugh necessarily meant anything more than the *sensus* viewed in the light of the total work and of any other relevant knowledge which the expositor could bring to bear upon it. There is no evidence that he regarded allegorical interpretation as having any necessary connection with the exposition of the *sententia.*

It is perhaps significant in this connection that in his *Epistle to Can Grande* Dante approaches his own work by a process similar to what Hugh is describing. He gives what he calls an *expositio secundum litteram* of the first lines of the *Paradiso.* First there is a Latin translation. This expounds the *littera* and the *sensus,* which Dante does not distinguish. He then explicates his meaning in more philosophic terms and cites relevant passages from scripture, Richard of St. Victor, St. Bernard, and St. Augustine. He refers to this exposition as an *expositio sententiae.* There is no question here of allegorical interpretation or hidden meaning.[26]

In short, Hugh's triad, *littera, sensus, sententia,* is simply a short description of the procedure any philologian necessarily adopts when he approaches a text, sacred or profane. It has no connection with the other triad, historical, allegorical, tropological. The latter applies only to scripture.

In Hugh's own century the more literary approach to the study of religion which he championed was yielding to an approach based on dialectic and a rational interpretation of the data of faith. What has been called "symbolic theology" was being replaced by scholastic theology. Thomas Aquinas is the inevitable choice as the spokesman for the new age. We are considering the general meaning of a total tradition and as an exponent of that tradition Thomas is beyond compare. He was, to be sure, accused by contemporary opponents of violent innovation. It is clear today, however, that his innovations were philosophical rather than theological. He substituted an Aristotelian for a Platonic idiom in the discussion of doctrinal problems, but his theology is conservative and mainly Augustinian. Aware of the exigencies of the age, Thomas's chief interest lay in a dialectical (i.e. a Hellenic) consideration of doctrine. Yet few theologians have been more completely aware of or handled more profoundly than he that tension between the Hellenic and the Hebraic, the universal and the concrete, or, to use his own terms, between essence and existence, which has dominated the Western theological tradition.

Thomas's treatment of exegesis, which, of course, is a part of theology, is a case in point.[27] In his handling of the exegetical tradition Thomas makes no innovations. He simply restates with the precision which his superior dialectical equipment makes possible the main lines of the doctrine of the Western Fathers, particularly Augustine, and of the more serious medieval teachers such as Hugh of St. Victor. Thomas adopts the terminology traditional since Cassian.[28] Scripture has four meanings, literal or historical, allegorical, tropological or moral, and anagogical. These meanings, however, are not all on one plane. There are two classes. The literal or historical forms a class by itself; the others are all members of a second class, the spiritual or mystical.

Like Jerome, Augustine, and Hugh, Thomas insists with great emphasis on the primacy of the literal sense. Only the literal sense can be used in establishing secure doctrinal positions. The mystical senses cannot be made a basis for doctrinal discussion.[29] In the establishment of the literal meaning one must, of course, consider the context and the *genre* of the text under consideration, thus arriving at what Hugh of St. Victor and Dante called the *sententia*. The literal or historical meaning is not necessarily, however, the same as what medieval literary theorists called the "proper" meaning. In the case of metaphors, it is, to use our own jargon rather than Thomas's, the tenor and not the vehicle which constitutes the literal meaning.[30] The words *Dextera Domini fecit virtutem,* for example, mean according to the letter, "The power of the Lord has worked a wonder." The phrase *dextera Domini* is only a poetical device for speaking of the divine power. God, being incorporeal, has no right hand, and scripture is not saying that He has. Such metaphors can be found in all poetry, and the inspired authors' way of speaking is often poetical.

The spiritual senses are something quite different from metaphor. They have nothing directly to do with words or meanings. They are derived from the things—events, persons—signified by the literal sense. "When the things of the Old Law signify the New, there is an allegorical meaning; when things done by Christ or the *figurae* of Christ [the just who preceded Christ] are signs of what we ought to do, there is a moral [or tropological] meaning; finally, if one regards these things as pointing to eternal glory, there is an anagogical meaning."[31] The whole spiritual meaning of scripture is dominated by an historical drive. "In holy scripture, later events are commonly signified by earlier ones; therefore, whenever scripture says something in the literal sense about an earlier event, that may be interpreted spiritually about later events, but the converse is not true."[32] A spiritual interpretation, then, is never the interpretation of a book. There is no question whatever of literary method. The scriptural interpreter is attempting to penetrate the significance of events moving in time. Scripture is a divinely inspired guide to those events where significance is most fruitfully to be sought.

Since real events are the basis of scriptural interpretation and real events can be produced only by divine power, it would seem to follow that there can be no spiritual or mystical level of meaning in the work of any uninspired author. That is, in fact, Thomas's conclusion. He draws it in considering the question whether mystical senses may be found in writing outside the Bible. The answer is an emphatic negative. In uninspired writing there is only one sense, the literal. This may be expressed either directly or metaphorically.[33] All that is involved is a choice of literary method.

In this opinion, Thomas is not an innovator. He introduces his answer with a quotation from Gregory the Great: "Holy Scripture transcends all sciences and teachings even in the very manner of its speaking; for, in one and the same statement, while it narrates an event, it sets down a mystery."[34] A similar idea is expressed by John of Salisbury in the *Polycraticus:*[35] "In the liberal disciplines [i.e. secular studies as opposed to theology] where only words are meaningful, not things, whoever is not content with the plain literal meaning seems to me to go astray or to be desirous of misleading his hearers and of keeping them from understanding the truth." God's events, in short, are mysterious; men's words should be clear.

Thomas is our last *point d'appui,* but the conclusion of a paper limited to the establishment of *points d'appui* around which little ground has been reconnoitred and none cleared must necessarily be a conclusion in which nothing, or very little, is concluded. Perhaps the following observations are permissible:

1. The better schooled commentators on the exegetical tradition, those who are doctrinally of greatest authority and most important from the point of view of the cultural historian, Jerome, Augustine, Hugh of St. Victor, Thomas, insist unanimously on the primacy of the letter as the only sound basis for doctrinal

development and for any further spiritual interpretation. The talk about the letter that killeth, the fruit and the chaff, is characteristic of the outbursts of hard-pressed Iron Age rhetoricians. Such statements should not be used to characterize the exegetical tradition as a whole. When they occur in the work of more serious expositors the context should, in each case, be carefully examined.

2. There is little in the exegetical tradition which would contravene the doctrine standard in the arts program of the medieval schools that the writer ought to produce a work which is not only clear but beautiful *secundum litteram*. Nor is there anything in the exegetical tradition to excuse the modern medieval scholar from the philologian's primary and basic task of laying bare the *prima facie* meaning of the work he is considering.

3. A clear distinction should be made between the "existential" or typological method of Christian exegesis and the allegorical method of Greek exegesis. It is the first that is dominant in the exegetical tradition as expounded by the best minds. Typology is also basic to the Western liturgies. The Christian insistence on the importance of the individual fact, person, or event might turn imaginative writers towards realism rather than allegory. Realism is, in any case, a notable feature of medieval drama, which is liturgical in origin, and of the imagination of many medieval writers, including, in my opinion, Langland. When the modern critic turns, like Keats's Apollonius, a cold philosophical eye on poor Kit and Kalotte dissolving them into *intellectus* and *memoria,* he is following Stoic rather than Christian methods of exegesis.

4. American medieval studies owe a real debt of gratitude to the critics of what I have called the pan-allegoric school. The

school has called vigorous attention to the importance of patristic and medieval exegesis for the interpretation of medieval letters. Their approach has shed much light and promises to shed more. When useful pioneering is accomplished, it is easy to be charitable if the pioneers, like the divines of the Iron Age, have their own heightened and telling way of putting things.

FOLKLORE, MYTH, AND RITUAL

Francis Lee Utley

"Mythic" approaches have the enthusiastic acclaim of many modern critics. They are no doubt as new as existentialism, but then they are also almost as old as human existence. For modern scholarship the role of folklore, myth, and ritual began with Jacob and Wilhelm Grimm, whose insights and errors are much like those of very recent scholars and critics. What should concern us is the pouring of new wine into old bottles, and remembering the real point of Jesus's parable, that the old goatskins were likely to split with the new ferment, one will agree that there is plenty of explosive yeast in the subject today.

I will begin with the most explosive term of all, myth, which at times bids fair to disrupt the ancient citadels of learning. Probably there is nothing in Philip Young's suggestion that the original root, *mü,* means a cow's mooing;[1] that sounds like the canard of some tired classicist striving to keep Australian bull-roarers and Hindu elephant gods out of Olympus. But the Greeks did give us the word, and it is chastening to realize what they gave us. Liddell and Scott provide many neutral meanings of *mythos:* "anything delivered by word of mouth, word, speech, counsel, command, promise, design, plan, the thing told, saying," and then as only one of many "a professed work of fiction, or one which bears a fabulous character, a tale, story, fable." *Logos* had a similar beginning, and even to the philosophers it became merely something like "reason, reflection." But we all know what the Gospel of John made of *logos,* and we should not be surprised to find that myth now has many meanings—political, social, religious, psychologically compulsive. The main problem is to keep them clear. It might have been better if, invaded by the thought of Freud, Jung, and Cassirer, we had kept the word *mythos* for these extended modern meanings and used the old word *myth* for such innocent tales as Pandora's box, Niobe's tears, Athena's spider, and Leda's egg-born babes. Nor should I mind employing it for Thor's hammer, Manibozho's earth-diving birds, Krishna's wooings, or the Hawaiian Maui's cosmic pranks. Northrop Frye's reminder that Aristotle's *Poetics* uses the word simply for "plot" [2] should bring us back to a clean, well-lighted place in spite of the surrounding *nada.* But I doubt whether many critics would allow that myth means merely what Ransom calls "structure"; the *nada* wells out of us all, though perhaps out of some of us more than others. Erich Fromm, indeed, seems to think that it may be controlled, that reason need not be wholly given up in spite of the dragon of the irrational.

At the moment I will not emulate St. George, but turn instead to some of the places where medieval scholars and critics have found mythical approaches useful. St. George himself is a case in point. Though his acts are as old as the fourth century A.D., the dragon did not appear till the twelfth, which leads the editors of *Butler's Lives of the Saints* to question the easy equation with Theseus's Minotaur and Hercules's Hydra.[3] But dragons live underground and myth, as we know, does likewise —Douglas Bush, somewhat wryly, has found it even in Jane Austen. We may sample its place in three profitable environments—*Beowulf, Sir Gawain and the Green Knight,* and Chaucer.

In 1909 W. W. Lawrence gave the *coup de grâce* to heavy German investigations which made too much of Scyld of the Sheaf and the Barley-God Beowa, by showing these genealogies to be wholly imported and fictitious.[4] Indeed, *Beowulf* is a paradox—though everyone today finds more pagan myth in everything, in *Beowulf* we find more Christianity. But scholar-critics are always venturesome, and in 1938 appeared J. R. R. Tolkien's "Beowulf, the Monsters and the Critics," which R. W. Chambers called "the finest appreciation which has yet been written of our finest Old English poem."[5] Tolkien argues that the poem is unified by the symbolic meaning of the combats with the monster Grendel, Grendel's dam, and the dragon, that the monsters are hence no blemish on the poem but a token of the evil with which man must contend in this transitory life. Of late this view has been queried by T. M. Gang, who asserts that dragons were real to the Anglo-Saxons and therefore much like human foes, and that Tolkien's symbolism will not survive a careful study of the text itself.[6] Gang was answered by Adrien Bonjour, who opposed the kingly halls of Hrothgar and Beowulf to the dark lairs of the monsters—the clean, well-lighted place to the *nada*. "On the face of it," says Bonjour, "there is no legerdemain in presenting Beowulf's struggle against the monsters as a fight against forms of evil," and to Gang's contention that the dragon has a moral right to attack the Geats, he counters that "there is a singularly striking disproportion here between offence and retribution, between the casual stealth of a precious cup by a stray wanderer in Dragonland, and the havoc wrought by the raging monster, applying indiscriminate scorched-earth tactics to the four corners of Geatland." [7] What none of them says exactly is that the problem of evil is a many-faceted one—that man's anxiety is just as great if he is attacked by the irrational race of Cain, or repaid like Adam for his own sins, or forced like Beowulf and Christ to atone for the sins of others. The poem is no more didactic than the Book of Job; it creates a "myth" in the modern sense like the battle between Ahab and Moby-Dick—a work of art which plumbs the depth of man's evil and the evil round him, in which all the actors are ambivalent because man himself is a complex of conflicting desires. Once, inspired by Tolkien and in the toils of the monster known as American Literature, I was tempted to write a paper called "Which Monster Do You Prefer?" My general idea was that Anglo-Saxons could write about the problem of evil as well as Melville could. But knowing that Beowulf died to protect his people, I chose Falstaff's way of discretion, and left the paper unwritten.

The basic contrast of courtly hall and wasteland monster exists again in *Sir Gawain,* though if there is any meaning in the terms, *Beowulf* is tragedy and *Sir Gawain* comedy. The mythographers have had a field day with Gawain. Even Northrop Frye reflects their theories. Speaking of spirits of nature who represent "moral neutrality" and "a world of mystery which is glimpsed but never seen," he says "Kipling's Mowgli is the best known of the wild boys; a green man lurked in the forests of medieval England, appearing as Robin Hood and as the knight of Gawain's adventure." I detect in Frye's language some humorous reserve—something less than the commitment which in Angus Wilson's *Anglo-Saxon Attitudes* led a lady historian and others to pious fraud in the name of the phallic god.[8] John Speirs's article on Gawain in *Scrutiny* led to much controversy. Speirs is our most unreconstructed "anthropological" critic—a man with flair and style and insight, and with the typical bad manners towards textual scholarship which seems to admit one to literary circles and the mystic halls of Faber and Faber. Gawain, to Speirs as to Jessie Weston, is "the hero, the agent who brought back the spring, restored the frozen life processes, revived the god—or (in later versions) cured the king."[9] He is a little more convincing when he moves from sources and positive statement to a literary judgment: "The fundamental knowledge in the poem, the hidden source which the poet has tapped, the ultimate source of the poem's actuality, strength and coherence, is the knowledge . . . that there is life inexhaustible at the roots of the world even in the dead season, that there is perpetually to be expected the spring re-birth."[10] He was anticipated by that rationalist Shelley, who said "If Winter comes, can Spring be far behind?" Both Speirs and Shelley have fine rhetoric and probably some truth. But of course there will be some who think of Gawain's testing and initiation as something wholly different—as that of a clever courtier who treads the sword-bridge between discourtesy to a lady, disloyalty to his host Bercilak, and the chastity which he wishes not to violate;

a courtier who learns that if one makes compromises one can be nicked by the nicor's ax; a highly sophisticated hero in a poem composed for the baronial courts which loved alliteration and love-problems; a hero with whom we identify, even today, not merely because of the racial unconscious but also because he sprang out of his guilt-complex with such comic aggressiveness. Ritual underlies comedy as well as tragedy, but comedy is *not* tragedy. And the irrationality of Gawain is violence, the disruption of courtly and individual order, rather than fertility ritual.

Ironically enough, one of the textual scholars whom Spiers belittles is Tolkien, who had probed the symbolic depths of *Beowulf*. And many writers had proceeded Speirs in their concern with Green Man and Wasteland. We may dismiss Jessie Weston, whose use as a source for Eliot's *Wasteland* has made her a kind of untouchable White Goddess herself. There was bound to be a reaction against George Lyman Kittredge's assured statement that

> Neither the Irish author . . . nor any of his successors in the line had any notion of associating the challenger with Celtic "probably arboreal" deities, Arician groves, spirits of vegetation, or the annual death and rebirth of the embodied vital principle. To them he was merely an enchanter, a shape-shifter, or else a human being under spells, and they wasted neither ink nor oil in mythologizing. And so we may drop this question into limbo, with the parting observation that thought is free.[11]

In 1935 William A. Nitze agreed with Kittredge that the Irish *Champion's Bargain* need not be a fertility myth, but argued that in the *Perlesvaus* there were traces of a "myth in which year after year a golden chapleted god is slain, and thereby his successor renews the fertility of the land and the welfare of the folk." Mythology can be abused, he thinks, but he believes that he does not abuse it.[12] Two years later A. H. Krappe dismissed Nitze contemptuously in a footnote as reviving outworn and untenable hypotheses, and urged that the Green Knight was a Celtic Lord of Hades.[13] He was more polite to Kittredge (one usually was in those days), but he opposed Kittredge's key point, that the knight is not green in the Emerald Isle, with the statement that this is an *argumentum ex silentio*. The appeal to the illogic of an opponent's *argumentum ex silentio* is safer, by the way, when one does not have an argument on hand oneself—the well-known rule of evidence, that the absence of a document does not prove that the fact never existed, cannot be reversed to prove that the absence of the document demonstrates the absent fact. The logical value of an appeal to silence is much more valuable when one is qualifying one's own position than when one is criticizing another's.[14] To Krappe green does not mean fertility, it means death. Apparently it can mean just about anything, and D. W. Robertson has chastened us a little by suggesting that the greenness of the devil in Chaucer's *Friar's Tale* is merely the proper color for a hunter, instead of the lingering memory of a Celtic otherworld.[15] Perhaps this would work as well for Robin Hood and Bercilak de Hautdesert, who were certainly as accomplished hunters of animals as the Summoner's smiling companion was of men.

But to Speirs the hunt itself is an archetype, and the three animals hunted by Bercilak, "the shy deer, the ferocious (yet courageous) boar, the cunning fox are the qualities of the natural man which Courtesy has to vanquish or, at least, civilize." On the Lady's first visit Gawain is shy, on the second he is morally courageous, and on the third he is overcome by a futile cunning when he takes the girdle and hides it. "The hunts move successively to a climax which is symbolic; the boar, we should think, would follow the fox, if the crescendo were literal-dramatic and not, as it is, spiritual-symbolic." [16] One presumes that Speirs got his theory from a similar one advanced in 1928 by Henry L. Savage,[17] but it is impossible to be sure, since the policy of writers for Faber and Faber is not to "smother the reader with footnotes" or to tell where one borrows one's ideas. Savage's authority in hunting matters is hard to impugn, and the poem gains in depths of character and structure by the suggestion. Yet I have often thought that this interpretation of the climax might co-exist with another, more purely symbolic of the noble tastes of the audience—the deer, being mere venison and a common source of food, is the minimal goal for a hunter; the boar, being both food and a test for martial valor, is much better; but best still, vermin or not, is the fox, who leads one on a merry chase to no purpose at all except the sheer sport of it. It is a truly aristocratic sport, as Oscar Wilde said: "the English country gentleman galloping after a fox—the unspeakable in full pursuit of the uneatable." But perhaps this is to be a little modern and overstress the comic nature of the tale.

One of the best mythic treatments of *Sir Gawain* is by Charles Moorman, who responds to both Speirs and Heinrich Zimmer.[18] For Speirs he has several correctives—the Green Chapel, to

Speirs the "source of life," is to Gawain and Moorman the "corsedest kirk"; Speirs's phallic architecture is a real castle. "Gawain," says Moorman, "is indeed the hero, but he unfreezes no life-processes (he himself is almost frozen, as a matter of fact), revives no god, cures no king." Moorman notes that Zimmer makes the Green Knight Death and his wife Life (agreeing with Krappe rather than with Nitze). Green, says Zimmer, is the color of livid corpses, but apparently his sole example is from Tibetan art, and Moorman thinks, as we might with him, that green is fairly commonly associated with life in English poetry.

We might interpose our own remarks on Zimmer's *The King and the Corpse,* a fascinating book which tells lively tales with thorough satisfaction and then comments on them with strangely irrelevant appeals to Jungian depth. Since the work is posthumous, and edited by Joseph Campbell, it is not certain how much of the commentary is that of the distinguished orientalist author and how much that of the editor. Even Zimmer-Campbell admits that the "myth" of Gawain has been fairly completely revised in the light of a chivalric and Christian *milieu.* But what we see as center the book sees as periphery, which seems to me a violation of the critical principle of poem *qua* poem and an unfortunate appeal to the genetic fallacy. Its extraction of an elusive "center" seems just the opposite of the method of Tolkien's with *Beowulf;* Tolkien explains his poem by attacking the tendency to dismiss the dominant monsters, while Zimmer and Campbell explain their poem by appealing to hints and traces and analogues which are wholly marginal. While it may be just at times to probe beneath the surface of a tale for hidden meanings, any true assessment of the poem will place the surface itself, the major narrative, in the foreground of any such assessment.

To return to Moorman. Though stressing the differentia of literature rather than the similarities which comparative mythologists (and Jungians) admire, Moorman is ready enough to find a myth in *Sir Gawain*. But it must be a useful myth, and a functioning part of a work of high literary sophistication.

> In arriving at a statement of the probable theme of the poem, then, we must keep before us at least four major aspects of the form of the poem—the fact that the poem is a self-contained action, the fact that the poem follows in general outline the pattern of the hero's *rite de passage* [a journey from innocence to knowledge], the poet's balanced use of court life and nature description, and the prevailing contrast between the court of Arthur

and the court of Bercilak, which comes off much better.

So we have the theme once more which Bonjour found in *Beowulf:* a contrast between noble hall and wilderness, clean well-lighted place and *nada,* though there is plenty that is rotten in the state of Camelot. Charles Muscatine made much the same contrast between aristocratic ideal and worldly chaos in the *Knight's Tale,* in which Theseus represents order and Saturn chaos. This broad kind of myth, politically and socially fitting for the epochs in which these three poems were written, is as convincing as the too-compulsively urged phallic ritual, however ubiquitous it may be, is not. I would not be a prude in the presence of the phallus (or the delta), and it appears that the ritual, attested in certain climates in the open—at Cerne Abbas, with the Babylonian Ishtar as she dances the dance of the seven veils, in Melanesia and in the Dionysian revels, may continue to be enacted less openly in and for us all. But whether our wasteland of dry religion and a sterile culture is to be redeemed by substituting the witches' coven for the YMCA and Planned Parenthood is not yet clear, though we can see that plenty of academics feel this to be possible.

Despite Muscatine's sensitive argument, Chaucer, like Jane Austen, has not proved especially fertile ground for the mythographers. Perhaps this is why Speirs's book on non-Chaucerian poetry is more provocative and even more illuminating than his *Chaucer the Maker*. Though *Troilus* and the *Knight's Tale* are both full of classical machinery, they are able to move quite well on the human level. Except for a humorous and oblique use of the God of Love in the scene of Troilus's reversal in the temple of Palladion, which perhaps may be taken no more seriously than an arrow-pierced comic Valentine, the rascally gods Jove, Apollo, and Mars are kept out of the direct action of the poem. Venus and the Muses and Furies play their part in the invocations, but this again looks like proto-renaissance machinery. Were we to take seriously a tempting chart in Erich Neumann's *The Great Mother,* we might urge that Chaucer unconsciously has invoked the four kinds of mother goddess—the youthful and terrible mothers in Thesiphone and the other Furies (Neumann's Kali and Circe, though I don't know which of Chaucer's is young and which old), the good mother of the vegetation mysteries (Venus and Mary), and the inspiring mother of the Muses. Such unconscious symmetry would be no coincidence to the

Jungian. But I am chary of trespassing on such domains, since Neumann warns us in the preface that "in both a theoretical and a practical sense, it is very hard for those who have not experienced the reality of the archetype *by undergoing analysis* to understand what depth psychology means by an archetype,"[19] and I wouldn't want to blunder.

The *Knight's Tale* has ample machinery, with prayers to Mars, Venus, and Saturn, and a symmetrical treatment of character and action with relationship to them. But if one believes that Saturn really tripped up Arcite's horse because Venus was backing her man Palamon, one might consider that earthquakes happen and horses stumble all the time without divine intervention, and that Theseus's Prime Mover is clearly a more powerful force than these all-too-human deities. Chaucer knew that the classical romance was, after all, a form of history—he calls on Clio in the second book of the *Troilus,* and his very gods are touches of local color. He saves his real marvels for such an Arthurian tale as the Wife of Bath would tell, or for a piece of irony like the *Merchant's Tale,* in which Pluto and Proserpina comically interfere for their respective sexes. Symbolic depth does occur, I believe, in the *Clerk's Tale,* where patient Griselda with her little ox's stall and her Rachel's well bears more than one mark of the patient Virgin Mary.[20] *Troilus's* consummation scene is full of ritual, but it is held in check by comparison with the parallel consummation of Dido and Aeneas in their cave; both have a driving symbolic and causative storm without. Both Chaucer and Virgil faced a similar artistic problem—how to dignify an affair passionate, intense, extra-legal and transitory, and Virgil did it by invoking Hera with her torches to bless the mock-marriage. Chaucer does it by making Pandarus a most efficient priest—with cushion, candle, ring and altar, and all the ecclesiastical words the enthusiastic confidante can muster. If anyone wishes to find the *hieros gamos* in these scenes he is welcome to do so; as Kittredge says, "thought is free." But I would rather leave the sacred marriage to Asia Minor and non-chivalric cultures, where it belongs. Finally, Chaucer gives us profound symbolism, not allegory, in the *Pardoner's Tale,* a story which may owe its brilliant plot and striking effect on the reader to India, a land where symbolism is culturally integrated and a part of life external. Interpreters differ as to whether the Old Man whose palsied hand knocks on his Mother Earth is Death, Death's spy, or Age, but this merely demonstrates the open-ended nature of the symbolism.

It is plain that the phallic arguments, however deflected by Jungian and other refinements, derive most of their force from Sir James Frazer and the Cambridge Ritualist school which followed him. As often, literary critics lag a little behind their teachers from another discipline. I am all for anthropology in criticism, but I think it should be good anthropology. Of late there have been some striking shifts in the myth and ritual school, under the sharp prodding of Henry Frankfort and the wise synthesizing of Clyde Kluckohn. Kluckhohn, in his searching essay, "Myths and Rituals: A General Theory,"[21] recognizes that the roles of myth and ritual are interdependent and have a common psychological basis. But he demonstrates that there is no direct priority of ritual over myth, that the therapeutic nature of ceremonial may differ in various societies, since "the needs which are typical in one society may be the needs of only deviant individuals in another society." Frazer was his own best critic, and lamented that his Vergilian golden bough had better parallels in other lands than in Italy. There are plenty of concessions in the new edition of S. H. Hooke's *Myth and Ritual,*[22] which admits that Hooke's famous "ritual pattern" of death and resurrection, creation, ritual combat, sacred marriage, and procession was at first applied without sufficient differentiation to the opposing culture patterns of Egypt and Akkadia, and that it is something less than universal. S. G. F. Brandon in this volume notes that India and China are notable exceptions to the assumption that the ritual pattern "is the natural expression in cultic imagery and practice of human societies when living at a specific cultural level and faced with the common challenges of the agriculturalist's life." The Brahmans opposed the development of a ritual kingship in India, and the Chinese for some reason (possibly their Confucian hardheadedness) never produced the dying and rising god, the ritual combat, or the sacred marriage. E. O. James, another pillar of the same school, states flatly that "it has to be recognized that however closely myth and ritual may have been allied, the myth has been by no means always or merely the spoken part of a rite; and when the two have occurred together as an entity an ætiological element often can be detected. Though on the whole it would seem that the ritual aspect is the earlier and more fundamental, a considerable corpus of myths has occurred in a non-cultic context."[23] This is of course the way of scholarship—a theory rests on the basis of sound fact, new insight and self-correction. We suspect the theory when it is reductive and unitary—when it rules out rival schools absolutely, when it ritually and compulsively repeats the same arguments to whoever will listen, when it attacks opponents personally and as an opposing conspiracy.

Another dimension is added by a brilliant interpreter of T. S. Eliot's symbolism, Helen Gardner, who warns us that

> the critic or scholar has a different function from that of the artist or original thinker. One of his uses is to help to preserve the creative thought of his own day from provincialism in time, by keeping alive and available in his own age what is neglected or disparaged by those absorbed in the preoccupations of the hour. His humble task is to protect his betters from the corruption of fashions.[24]

In a similar vein Morton Bloomfield remarks that

> Unless the system implied by them really gives meaning to the world and man, the general, the cyclic, and the mythical are no more meaningful than the particular, the unique, and the fact. . . . The mere cycles of nature, for instance, are as meaningless as any unique fact unless one is satisfied by a purely biological vision of the world.[25]

One might glance at some salutary examples of the particular in the midst of myth found in the Bible. When Jesus (Mark 5.43) waked the synagogue ruler's twelve-year-old daughter from the sleep of death she arose and the spectators were moved with astonishment. "And he charged them straitly that no man should know it; and commanded that something be given her to eat." This last homely particular, the eating, raises the story into credibility, whether it be historical or literary. Again, when Jesus is taken in the garden his disciples flee (Mark 14.52). "And there followed him a certain young man, having a linen cloth cast about his naked body; and the young man laid hold on him: And he left the linen cloth, and fled from them naked." This "curious little incident" is peculiar among the four Gospels. It has been surmised that it might recall Joseph's escape from Potiphar's wife or be "more naturally interpreted as a personal experience of the evangelist, as his signature to his portrait of Jesus."[26] As critics we need not be concerned whether it was a confirmation of Old Testament prophecy or a sign of historicity and the eye-witness, or whether it reflects something like the loss of the old garments and the putting on of the new—what hits us between the eyes is the convincing quality of the vivid, irrelevant detail. Of such unlinked happenings is life made; all commentary is external to the work of art itself.

Such remarks as I have been making should not be taken as showing antagonism to such "mythic" criticism as illuminates the work of art, such as the penetrating studies by Lydenburg and Lewis on Faulkner's *The Bear*.[27] Anyone who has taught this story in the classroom knows that he must call upon every resource in anthropology, folklore, history, and human wisdom to create for the student a depth and response such as is the exhilarating reward of the teacher, as a woman's pleasure is to the man who is her sexual partner. But we know how conscious Faulkner's myths are, and we cannot here debate the old question of the difference between the post-Freudian author and the pre-Freudian, between the unconscious and the conscious unconscious in literature.[28]

The recent fashion of the use of patristic analogues (what is often called "Robertsonianism") in the interpretation of later medieval literature, Latin and vernacular, is in a sense opposed to the mythic fashion and in a sense much like it. It is opposed because it concerns itself with texts which may very well have been available to the medieval author, instead of with mythic memories which rationally would be repudiated by him. But it is like mythic criticism because it is revisionist, because it rests on hypothetical analogues rather than strict demonstration of tangible source, and because its lack of strict logic and method sometimes has a fatal appeal to the scholar in embryo. No sensible scholar today would ridicule the allegory which Christian commentators have forced upon the fertility ritual of the Song of Songs. By now the symbolism of Christ and Church is as potent as the sacred marriage with the girl whose "two breasts are like two young roes that are twins, which feed among the lillies"; and the "garden inclosed is my sister, my spouse; a spring shut up, a fountain sealed" may mean both what it meant in a land close to Ugarit and Canaan and what it meant to the medieval Churchmen who applied it to nuns and to the Blessed Virgin. The husks of an ancient ritual are not the rite itself, and if it is syncretized into a new ritual pattern the honest historian will not reject the emergent in favor of the traditional. To turn to another example, the serpent of Genesis, read as the devil, is in one sense a case of overreading, for it is clearly established that demonology in the modern meaning is a very late development in Hebrew belief. Yet in another sense, if the Babylonian parallels are correct and Rahab and Leviathan are Palestinian reflexes of the watery chaos Tiamat, who fought with the ordering god Marduk, there is a dualism in Genesis which makes the serpent akin to the medieval devil. The plain text of Genesis, of course, makes him only an etiological beast who stole man's immortality and can now cast his skin, and who was punished by god with the words "upon thy belly shalt thou go, and dust shalt thou eat all the days of thy life. . . . [Man's seed] shall bruise thy head, and thou shalt bruise his heel." Medieval commentators made this a prophecy of how the Virgin's Child would have revenge on the demon who misled Eve and brought death and sin to her children. All of these creations of intellectual history, Tiamat, crawling serpent, and Satan the enemy of the Virgin, are now relevant and emergent aspects of the fertile Biblical text. To reduce the text to merely one of these is treason for both critic and literary historian.

One or two other positive ritual elements in medieval literature deserve discussion—the folkplay and Robin Hood. Ludicrous as the antics of the performers now are in the modern texts, there seems to be no question that the folkplays preserve traces of some kind of sacred drama.[29] Speirs transfers this concedable point to the Towneley Plays, for which he feels the Mass and the Latin drama are not a sufficient source.[30] There may be something in his contention, since all elements in a culture pattern draw sustenance from one another. But when he argues that the "hornyd lad" which the shepherds find in Mak's cradle is the Horned God of Margaret Murray and the post-atomic covens we part company—that lad seems merely a sheep stolen by Mak and his maculate fingers. Buffoonery may have ritual significance, and then again it may not. One likes a genuine massing of evidence before succumbing to the witching words.

From the beginning Robin Hood has haunted the mythographers. He is a Green Man, he has ritual or some kind of combats, and he appears in folkplays (which by the way are remarkably without mystery). Thus presumably his universal appeal today is owing to this heritage. I doubt whether my childhood love for Robin Hood was unconscious phallicism, though I am quite willing to believe that I enjoyed his rebellion against authority. The debate goes on. In 1956 P. Valentine Harris revived the old notion that Robin was to be identified with a historic Robert Hood of Wakefield,[31] and D. N. Kennedy took the extreme myth-ritual view, that folklore has nothing to do with history,[32] a position best known from Lord Raglan's *The Hero*. I promise to demonstrate someday that Abraham Lincoln on Lord Raglan's premises did not exist, since he qualifies with some seventeen out of Raglan's twenty-two heroic traits which make up the "heroic pattern." Neither Harris nor Kennedy seems to realize that Robin Hood, like Lincoln, could be the product both of history and of popular belief. Bacil F. Kirtley, also in 1956, dismissed the various unitary theories of history, solar mythology, and witches' covens and rituals, and argued simply that Robin is the creation of popular fancy—and, we might add, popular wish.[33] This will not wholly satisfy those who wish to recapture the identification they had with Robin in their adolescent days of anger.

Worthy of attention is an amusing article by Daniel Hoffman called "The Unquiet Graves."[34] Hoffman, who established himself as a scholar by demonstrating the commercial frauds in the popularization of Paul Bunyan,[35] has also established himself as a very competent poet. He mutes his attack on Graves by dividing himself into his two *personae*. The Poet describes some of Graves's arguments, and the Professor agrees it is "certainly intriguing" and has "just enough plausibility in it to traduce my brightest students." But it is the Poet who shows that Graves is not above manufacturing a new text of *The Unquiet Grave* to prove his point. He sums up his ambivalences by saying of the Professor and Graves:

> You are absolute for the relative.
> He is resolutely for the absolute.
>
> Your world conforms to what the mind expects;
> His world soul's singleness of kind reflects.
>
> . . . . .
>
> I am relatively for the absolute.
> My mind sees many while my soul seeks one.
>
> To be a fabler in an age of fact
> Demands a stubborn stomach. Haut intellect
>
> And soul's intransigent passion may yet compose
> The resolute poem that threatens yet all our prose.

Though I hope I am not so prosaic as Hoffman's Professor, I should like to turn to a fairly prosaic problem, that of folklore method. The folklorist deals with more placid tales than the mythologist, and he seeks for authentic documents with the same care that the historian does. His documents present a special problem. Faced with the clutter of untestable definitions of folklore, I have chosen the one which helps best in the authentication of evidence—that folklore is "literature transmitted orally." [36] Ultimate origins are hard to prove, and it is not even certain who are the "folk," but we can all recognize oral transmission when we hear it. I have had a friendly private exchange or two on the subject with Roger Sherman Loomis, on the occasion of his recent article on "Arthurian Tradition and Folklore,"[37] in which he argues that most modern Arthurian folklore "survivals" are late and derivative and denies the assumption by Nutt and Weston that "certain of the great stories of the Matter of Britain originated in the fancies of plowmen, goose-girls, blacksmiths, midwives, or yokels of any kind." I think this is risky ground, a defense of the élite which led Hans Naumann and Lord Raglan to say that all folklore has an aristocratic origin. Loomis, I think, would not really want to be found in such company. His allegiance is rather to Joseph Bédier, who was skeptical about hypothetical "common sources" and the theories of *les folkloristes* in general. What Bédier really displayed was a keen eye to the documents, and that meant tangible literary sources and analogues rather than remote Oriental folk tales and lost *lais*. His brilliant example held French scholars in thrall for many years, so that until recently the orderly collection and classification of French folk tales lagged far behind that in other European countries.[38] By ignoring the true folk tales Bédier was very far from modern folklorists; by subjecting the literary documents to a critique he was very close to them.

The folklorist's first task is to decide which tale is oral and which is literary, and that means on the evidence before our own eyes. The oral tale is usually modern, and if properly collected it bears the stamp of collector, place, date, tale-teller, and provides the exact unaltered text. The literary tale has none of these clear signs of oral transmission. This leads us to a startling paradox—that most or all medieval "folk tales" are literary, since that is the only way in which they could have been preserved. In some ways they may be partly authenticated by internal evidence and external analogue, and they are important in the study of the history of the folk tale, above all for the age of the imbedded motifs, but to label them indiscriminately "folklore" is misleading. Nutt and Weston and Ward's *Catalogue of Romances* are all careless on this point. Stith Thompson's *Motif-Index* may seem so, since the parallels in literature to folkloristic motifs are often included, but if its relationship to the Aarne and Thompson type index is understood, no violation of scholarly rigor is evident.[39] No folk-tale "type" has been included in the latter which does not have a vigorous life in oral tradition. The kind of rigor of which I am speaking is akin to that of structural linguistics, which insists that the true record of speech can be found only in a corpus provided by modern techniques of phonetic transcription and tape-recording. Now this is not to say that Anglo-Saxons did not talk, or that their contemporaries did not tell folk tales. This would be to use the *argumentum ex silentio* with a vengeance. It merely means that we must be careful how we use our evidence.[40] Arthurian romances, and even their Celtic forebears, are highly sophisticated in form, tone, and intention, but the picture may be complicated by the fact that the *filid,* the bards and the minstrels delivered their tales and poems orally. And the performers and their audience may have been closer to the goose-girls than T. S. Eliot or even Allan Ginsberg would like to be.

One must, therefore, be very careful what he calls the folklore sources of a medieval literary document. Casual appeal to "oral tradition" can be, even more than appeal to an identifiable written source, a device to slow down genuine criticism, genuine consideration of the poet's own creativity. Gerould has shown this with the Old English *Guthlac A*.[41] The art of Chaucer's Nun's Priest and Robert Henryson's *Fables* can best be understood by appeal to a written *Roman de Renart* or *Reinecke Fuchs*,[42] rather than by reference to absent folk tales. The fact that most of the folk-tale types which Chaucer shares with Boccaccio's *Decameron* are clearly not borrowed from Boccaccio is an important piece of literary history. But this does not prove that he borrowed them from folklore, though it makes the theory possible. Friedrich Panzer has demonstrated *Beowulf's* similarity to some two hundred versions of the Bear's Son tale (Aarne and Thompson Tale-Type 301),[43] and Rhys Carpenter has argued that the *Odyssey* is closely related to the same tale.[44] But both Panzer and Carpenter lapse from strict method—in the use of literary vs. oral documents, in the confusion of tale with motif, and in the failure to use the oikotypal approach, that is, the special study of versions close in locale to the basic literary work under examination.

There are many places where folkloristic procedures and information can help the medievalist. Arthur Moore has shown that Dunbar's *Twa Mariit Wemen and the Wedo* may owe its bawdry and its indiscretion to the revels of St. John's Eve.[45] His *Secular Lyric in the Middle Ages* and Richard Leighton Greene's *The Early English Carols* make valuable use of modern oral parallels of medieval song.[46] It is somewhat disappointing to find that all Speirs can contribute on that richly literary and folkloristic poem, *The Owl and the Nightingale,* is a footnote making the combat of Summer and Winter the central theme.[47] None of us would deny the Summer-Winter, "fair and foul weather fight together" tradition, but we might recall that the best-known medieval version, a *Contentio,* was from the hand of the austere Alcuin. D. W. Robertson argued that the center of that haunting poem, "Maid in the Moor Lay," is someone like the Virgin,[48] but Richard Greene has shown that Bishop Richard de Ledrede in the fourteenth century composed a pious parody of it and considered it a wholly profane song.[49] The key to the mystery may lay in folk belief. To those who hold the Raglan position that folklore excludes history we might counter not only with Lincoln but with Eleanor of Castile, who became a demon queen and swan-maiden shortly after her death in 1304, long before the romance of *Richard Coeu de Lion.*[50] Anna J. Mill has noted the folk-tale sources of the Devil's association with Noah's Wife in the Newcastle *Noah's Play,* which had formerly been the center of much fantastic speculation about the evolution of the "Vice."[51] I have just read a paper at the Kiel Folk-tale Congress on the story, "The Devil in the Ark," which lies behind the English play—its antecedents are clearly in Eastern Europe.[52] Miss Mill as a literary historian was shedding light on a literary document; I, as a folklorist for the moment, was concerned primarily with the oral variants themselves, localized and mapped and dated, and in whatever accurate picture one could draw of the origin and history of the folktale, its wanderings and cultural transmission. There is much common ground, but the two roles are different. C. Grant Loomis, in his *White Magic,* has discussed the folklore elements in the lives of the saints.[53] There is much cultural breadth which might be gained by a comparison of Christian with Jewish legends. For instance, there is a charming story of a Jew who did not know how to pray and who therefore jumped over a ditch in honor of God, an interesting analogue to that most medieval of all legends, the *Jongleur of Notre Dame*.[54] The remarkable identification of poet, man, cross, and Christ in the *Dream of the Rood* is fundamentally an Anglo-Saxon poetic creation, but as I have shown elsewhere it has its folkloristic and oriental analogues.[55]

My emphasis in this paper on the value of the individual and the particular is not meant to oppose all theorization about the symbolic and the general. Theories are one arm of scholarship, and my attitude towards them is in some measure temperamental. Some deplore all generality, others admire it. Of those who seek the general some, like the solar mythologists and the less careful followers of Frazer and Jung, seek broad origin theories to take the place of history, while others, like the Russian formalist V. Propp[56] and the structural linguists, seek descriptive and predictive formulas which are constantly alterable and verifiable by the latest accession of facts. Once generality is achieved, some will be content with the description and others, like the Jungians and the applied anthropologists, will wish to "make it useful." Everyone will know where his place is in this grouping, and it would be futile for me to try to argue that any one of these positions is best. Yet I like to be clear. It would have been safer in this paper to cover some group—folklorists, mythic critics, or literary historians—with obliquity, or to take refuge myself in obliqueness, a common gambit for academicians unwilling to commit themselves today. But I believe that clarity is possible even in an age of depth psychology, content analysis which impugns each man's "bias," and periodic witchhunts.

The search for myth and the search for sources in literature seem to me to be equally relevant to the work of art. The search for sources, handled well, seeks to understand poetic process by juxtaposing an original to a derivative, the latter often but not always a better work of art. The search for myths seeks to understand why works of art transcend the ages, and, handled well, it provides a structure for discussion and analysis. Many mythographers and their critics fall into a common error, that of assuming that mythic criticism is a search for historical origins. As Frye says, "To the literary critic, ritual is the *content* of dramatic action, not the source or origin of it. . . . It does not matter two pins to the literary critic whether such a ritual had any historical existence or not." [57] And one of the better Jungians, Erich Neumann, makes it clear that "psychohistory" is not chronological history.[58] Folklorist and mythographer are not in opposition, though their methods differ; the one is primarily concerned with individuality among the similarities of folk tale or ballad, the other with similarity among the individualities. Serious folklorists tend to be somewhat positivist, because there is so much positive work to do in their extensive field. Yet, as Frye says again, "It is clear that archetypes are most easily studied in highly conventional literature; that is, for the most part, naïve, primitive, and popular literature. In suggesting the possibility of archetypal criticism, then, I am suggesting the possibility of extending the kind of comparative and morphological study now made of folktales and ballads into the rest of literature." [59]

As for the war between Poet and Professor, we may say that the tradition of scholarly accuracy, with all its pitfalls, is at least as noble a tradition as Yeats's line of Irish protestant writers or

Graves's white daisy chain. "Facts" in literature are not unsupported conjectures about sources, biography, or *milieu*—they are what we really know about these things and their relevance to the poem; and the central fact is the poem itself, what can be made of its plain sense and its irrational contradictions by reasonable and perceptive men. If the vegetation myth is useful we may use it, but if it becomes vitiated by overuse, a cliché of scholarship, then we should relegate it to limbo with Max Müller's Sun God. Facts, like common words as opposed to clichés, are never vitiated or commonplace; they are always the germ from which can spring new and fresh understanding. Since much of what is said in the name of mythic criticism is said in the name of Kierkegaard and a general modern reaction against eighteenth-century rationalism, nineteenth-century positivism, and twentieth-century world politics, it should be said that a *religion manqué* (Herbert Weisinger once gave me the phrase) is no substitute for either religion or science. Pascal, who had in Chateaubriand's words "completed the circle of the human sciences" by the age of twenty-three, turned to religion. This might seem an argument for the vanity of the sciences, including historical sciences like folklore and literary history. It seems to me better taken as a parable for learning the sciences before one transcends them.

CLASSICAL FABLE AND ENGLISH POETRY IN THE FOURTEENTH CENTURY

Richard Hamilton Green

AMONG THE ISSUES in current medieval literary studies none has aroused more interest, or sharper differences, than the interpretation of conventional images and themes in late medieval poetry. I should like to take up a very limited aspect of this complex problem and, because the topic is a matter of controversy, to bespeak your benevolent attention to the carefully limited claims and suggestions I shall presently make. The attitudes expressed in this paper, both in their estimate of the importance of certain kinds of medieval learning for the reading of poetry and in their application by way of example, may justly be found to represent a trend in current medieval literary studies. If so, the tendency embraces a very wide range of critical interests and assumptions, and I have tried to define my own position with some care. I hope that it will not be confused with what is taken to be the position of others on related matters in the interpretation of medieval poetic figures.

Within the large area of conventional images and narrative

themes used by the poets to convey, enrich, and decorate their own original experience, I shall limit my attention to images derived from the fables of the pagan poets as these were interpreted and exploited by fourteenth-century scholars and poets. My approach to the problem will be largely historical and theoretical: I shall first review the status of mythological study in the fourteenth century, its assumptions and methods, and the implications it was found to have for classical and contemporary poetry. I shall go on to suggest some of the ways in which this historical information can be of use to the modern reader of medieval poetry. Such few examples as I offer will be taken from the poetry of Chaucer, though it will be clear that I regard the study of the mythological tradition as relevant to our understanding of medieval poetry in centuries other than the fourteenth and in languages other than English.

A new account of medieval attitudes toward the meaning and value of the fabulous persons and stories of the ancient poets may need some justification. In recent years we have seen an impressive number of studies in Renaissance and medieval literature and art devoted to the recovery of the figurative meanings of conventional imagery derived from the classical and biblical traditions. I have in mind particularly the work of Liebeschütz, Seznec, Auerbach, Panofsky, Curtius, D. W. Robertson, Wind, Mâle, D. C. Allen, Tuve, Singleton, and Osgood, among many others. In spite of obvious differences in the objects of their study, and of the variety of scholarly interests and critical attitudes they represent, these writers share a common concern for the identification of images and configurations of images in terms of the artistic and intellectual traditions in which conventional modes of representation enjoyed their continuing vitality. In the historical part of this paper I am indebted to these writers, as well as to the editors who have provided us with such modern critical texts as we have. It is significant that among these names, given mainly to place my subject in a context of study which I hope may extend its implications, the art historians and students of Renaissance literature occupy an important place. Readers of medieval poetry have much to learn from their work, particularly from their awareness of the medieval view of physical phenomena and historical events as the manifestation of invisible truth, and from their early recognition of the importance of the mythographers as sources of conventional interpretation useful in identifying figures and themes in the subject matter of medieval and Renaissance art.

Students of medieval poetry, however, and especially those interested in Middle English poetry, have almost wholly neglected this aid to interpretation, perhaps because they have been preoccupied by other useful—if often nonliterary—matters, or because they have regarded the English poet's use of classical figures and fables as a rather tiresome and shallow decorative convention. But the frequency, and indeed the conventionality, of classical allusion in Middle English poetry point to its importance as part of the language of representation, common to the poet and his experienced contemporary reader, which we ought to try to recover. For if we agree that the image is at the center of poetic expression, and that it derives part of its life within the unique context of the poem from another life in tradition outside the poem, we ought to assent to the probable usefulness of knowing as much as we can about that tradition.

When Chaucer's Knight relates that Theseus, riding out from Athens to conquer Thebes and kill the tyrant Creon, had borne before him a pennon "Of gold ful riche, in which ther was ybete The Mynotaur, which that he slough in Crete," we are given another ornament in the poem's richly decorated surface which has been so much and so justly admired. But the emblem of the Minotaur does more than decorate the text; it increases and refines the reader's awareness of the legendary hero's role in Chaucer's fable by recalling another famous instance of his prowess. When the image of the Minotaur, placed here in a new design of other images conventionally associated with Theseus, is understood as a mirror reflecting meanings traditionally attached to this fabulous event, its function in Chaucer's presentation of Theseus as preeminent in love and war can be more fully understood.

Before I am finished, I shall return to Theseus and the *Knight's Tale;* for the present, I mention him merely to illustrate my thesis in its simplest terms. When the hero of antique fable appears in a fourteenth-century poem, his name evokes the stories of his exploits as these were known to the poet and his readers; conventional detail becomes part of the data specifying the role of the hero in his new poetic existence. But more than the familiar stories are evoked; for the stories themselves were commonly understood to embody other, more profound and important, natural and moral meanings. The poet could adapt, reshape, rearrange the traditional images; he could not ignore or escape their suggestive power. I suggest that the modern reader ought to know the manifold meanings conventionally attached to these stories in the Middle Ages. For poetry so distant in time, and so different in its view of the world and of history, neither modern taste nor modern classical scholarship will be sufficient preparation. In popular modern usage the images of classical and biblical literature are not only trite but grossly changed. Giants and Titans have become the journalists' cliches for whatever is big and powerful, and so usually admirable. Shipowners, board chairmen, even the great who have gone before us in the academy are honored by the name. "There were giants in those days," has been the text for many a nostalgic speech, a transformation which would have evoked laughter or dismay in ages which knew mythology and the Scriptures better. Nimrod has become a hunter of ducks, not men; and teachers of Chaucer can be honored, without irony, as "myn owene maister deere."

By way of preface to my survey of fourteenth-century attitudes toward classical mythology, I should like to review some of the evidence on which it is based. The literature is massive and various; some of it is easily accessible in modern editions, but much of it is not. New manuscript material is regularly being turned up in British and Continental libraries, and much important critical and editorial work on the manuscripts remains to be done. The material I shall mention is, with a few exceptions, available in modern editions; most of the rest can be read in Renaissance editions.

From the early part of the century we have the work of the Italian humanists and poets: the verse epistles of Albertino Mussato defending the excellence and utility of ancient poetry against its scholastic detractors; the theory and practice of Dante in his *Convivio;* and the allegorical commentary on Ovid's *Metamorphoses* by their friend Giovanni del Virgilio. Still early in the century we find the monumental French commentary on Ovid, the *Ovide moralisé,* which contains long and valuable digressions on other fabulous narratives, notably on the *Thebaid* of Statius. A work of the same period, about 1330, but quite different in its selection and arrangement of the pagan stories, is *Fulgentius metaforalis* by the English Franciscan, John Ridewall. There are also commentaries on Virgil, one of which is attributed to the Englishman Nicholas Trivet. In 1342, Pierre Bersuire, French Benedictine and cardinal, friend of Petrarch and Philippe de Vitri, produced his full and very influential commentary on the *Metamorphoses* as the fifteenth book of his encyclopedic *Reductorium morale.* Bersuire's *Ovidius moralizatus,* or *De fabulis poetarum,* or *Metamorfosis Ovidiana moraliter explanata,* as it was variously called, must have been very popular in England if one can judge by the number of manuscripts and editions which attribute it to Thomas Walleys, Nicholas Trivet, and Robert Holkot.

Important evidence from the middle of the century is found in Richard de Bury's comments on the pagan poets in his *Philobiblion.* And from about the same period we have the brilliant defense of poetry by Petrarch in his *Familiar Letters* and the *Invective contra medicum,* as well as his practice in his poetry. Between 1363 and 1373, Giovanni Boccaccio produced his great encyclopedia of ancient mythology and fourteenth-century interpretation, the *Genealogy of the Gods.* In the first thirteen of fifteen books, Boccaccio assembles and arranges systematically the vast accumulation of classical legend, and, for many of the stories, supplies traditional—and sometimes original—figurative interpretations. In the final two books he presents his theory of poetry, incorporating and revising ideas he had expressed earlier in his *Vita di Dante,* his *Commento alla Divina Commedia,* and his literary correspondence. Shortly after the appearance of the *Genealogy,* in 1375, Giovanni de Bonsignore wrote his *Allegorie ed esposizioni delle metamorphosi,* a commentary to be found in the Rosenwald collection at Jenkintown. Finally, at the end of the century, and roughly contemporaneous with the most productive period of Chaucer's career, we have the work of the Italian humanist, Colluccio Salutati. In his *De laboribus Herculis,* he offers a defense of poetry, a presentation of poetic theory, and a rather full allegorical interpretation of the myths associated with Hercules. Moreover, many of the letters of his voluminous correspondence are concerned with poetry and mythology.

Nearly all of the works I have mentioned so far are concerned directly and principally with the interpretation of myth, either as commentaries on Ovid or as collections and interpretations of the fables of the poets generally. There is, however, other evidence which bears on the use of mythology in fourteenth-century art and literature. Such evidence is found in a class of works usually called "moralities," of which the popular *Liber de exemplis* of John of San Geminiano and the *Moralitates* of Robert Holkot are representative. Evidence of primary importance is, of course, to be found in the poetry of the century, especially when, as with Dante's *Commedia,* the poetry became the object of commentary within the century.

I have so far mentioned only works written during the fourteenth century, but I should add that these works are the products of a tradition of more than a thousand years, and that the authorities on which they were based were themselves still widely read. I need only mention such major *auctores* as Macrobius, Martianus, and Servius; Lactantius, Isidore, and Rabanus; Fulgentius, Remigius, and Lactantius Placidus; to give some idea of the history which lay behind the late medieval mythographers. In the immediate background of the works I have cited is Mythographus III, almost certainly the English scholar Alexander Neckam, writing about 1200, and the Ovidian commentators of the twelfth and thirteenth centuries: Arnolf of Orleans, Albrecht von Halberstadt, and John of Garland.

It may be useful to look briefly at the theory of poetry and its interpretation which is responsible for this body of mythological commentary. For humanists like Boccaccio and Salutati poetry was a marvelous and mysterious art, important in itself and as a means of expressing profound truth; for the moralists, like Bersuire, it seems to have been relatively unimportant in itself, but useful as a means of presenting moral truths in an appealing way. Poetry, writes Boccaccio, is a kind of fervor, a rare and divine gift of exquisite invention and exquisite expression. This fervor is sublime in its effects, impelling the soul to a longing for utterance; it produces strange, original creations of the mind, composes them in a certain order, adorns them with a unique fabric of words and meanings, and in this way covers the truth with a fabulous and fitting veil (*Genealogy* XIV.vii). Of the pagan poets he remarks that "though they were not Catholics, they were so gifted with intelligence that no product of human genius was ever more skillfully enveloped in fiction, nor more beautifully adorned with exquisite language than theirs" (*Genealogy,* Proem). Of his own commentary in the *Genealogy* he says: "my interpretations will enable you to see not only the art of the ancient poets, and the relations of the false gods, but natural truths hidden with an art that will surprise you" (*ibid.*).

Salutati tries to fix more precisely the poetic principles of delight and instruction. Song, he says, is the essence of poetry, not invention which is shared with orators and philosophers. Poetry captures its audience with a double pleasure, so mysterious that it can scarcely be understood. The melody is one source of pleasure, but the other and highest pleasure comes from a *mirabilis concinna mutatio* of words and things and events. It is this marvelous, perfectly fitted transformation of one thing into another that constitutes the essence of poetry and the source of its greatest pleasure. This change, Salutati goes on, is not merely a matter of elegant diction, a change of words for words. Poets indeed use such tropes, but so do others. The poets change things for things, *res vero pro rebus,* and this mode of figurative discourse belongs peculiarly to them (*De laboribus Herculis* I.ii). Salutati offers the example of the golden bough in the sixth book of the *Aeneid:* that branch which the Sibyl warned him to break off before he went down into the underworld signified the tree standing before Diana's temple, or the virtues of Pythagorean wisdom which are necessary if man is to emerge from his descent into the world, or riches which excite desires which can drive men to hell, or wisdom itself, which is as shining and incorruptible as gold, and which, like the fabulous tree, is not diminished by yielding part of itself.

If delight in penetrating the beautiful and enigmatic fiction constituted the essence of poetic experience, as distinguished from other kinds of knowing, the truth presented by the poet and found by the reader constituted its justification. Every considerable discussion of poetry in the fourteenth century repeats the famous dicta of Horace: The source of all good writing is wisdom; the poet's aim is to teach or please, or to combine that which delights with that which is useful in life. The poet who mixes the useful with the pleasurable achieves his purpose by charming his reader and at the same time instructing him. This conventional attitude may be illustrated by a passage from Salutati which also shows the late fourteenth-century writer's keen sense of the long tradition in which he was working (*Prima editio,* 4–6):

> No one should suppose that the sacred poets, *qui aut prodesse volunt aut delectare poete, ut Flaccus ait, aut simul et iocunda et idonea dicere vite,* left us their fables of gods and men with the intention that their stories should be believed or imitated. For no poet wishes to do harm, and what greater harm could they do than persuade credulous men to mistake vain and false things for true. . . . Something wholly different was hidden (and is still hidden) beneath the surface of the fables which they artfully composed, so that, although they may deceive the ignorant with a certain pleasure, they offer to wiser readers the fragrant odor and sweet taste of inner meaning. Whoever does not believe this should read Cicero's *De Natura Deorum* and *De Divinatione;* and let him read Macrobius, Lactantius, Fulgentius, Alexander, and the many other authorities who have discovered the hidden secrets of these fables. Let them read, too, the admirable work my wise fellow countryman, Giovanni

> Boccaccio, *The Genealogy of the Gods,* in which Boccaccio wonderfully improved on the traditional interpretations of all the older writers on this subject. Unless I am mistaken, doubters will be ashamed of their incredulity and struck with admiration for the poets and their fables. Finally, those who deny allegorical meanings in the traditional stories of the poets do not, in the words of the great Lactantius, understand the way poetic freedom works and how far the poet may go in his art, since the office of the poet is to change what really happened into new forms by means of oblique configurations and a certain beauty.

For those mythographers who were less interested in the delights of poetry, the hidden truth and its uses for edification were enough. As Bersuire puts it, the fables of the poets are like the Egyptian treasures and the pagan women of the Old Testament, useful for the building of the temple of learning and the increase of the chosen people in virtue (*Reductorium morale,* Prologus). This diversity of attitude accounts in part for the variety of the mythological works. Some were composed for the sake of the ancient poetry, and for the use of contemporary poets and readers, and in these the literal fable and its historical background are treated at length. Others seem designed to provide the teacher and preacher with elegant and familiar moral examples. They have in common the primary concern for the truth which was discovered in the fiction; and for us they have a common usefulness in providing us with the conventional meanings and values which were then evoked by the fables.

Methods of interpretation, especially in their theoretical formulations, show the same unity of basic intent in the midst of variety of emphases. When the humanist wanted to stress the divine origins of pagan poetry and the spiritual value of the truth enveloped in its fictions, he described a method of analysis derived from, and bearing important analogies to, the traditional fourfold method of biblical exegesis. Thus Boccaccio, early in the *Genealogy,* gives this account of his method: "You should know that in these fictions there are more meanings than one; indeed, they can be called polyseme, that is, manifold in meaning. The first sense is found in the cortex, and this is called the literal sense; the others are found in the things signified by the literal meaning, and these are called the allegorical senses" (I.iii). He illustrates his method with the victory of Perseus over the Gorgon and his flight into the heavens. The *moralis sensus* is the wise man's victory over vice and his ascent to virtue. *Allegorice,* the fable signifies the mind's contempt for earthly delights and its elevation to celestial things. Anagogically we discover in the victory of the hero Christ's conquest of the prince of this world and his ascent into heaven. Boccaccio concludes by saying that he has no intention of interpreting the fables in all these senses. This is strikingly verified in the chapter devoted to Perseus much later in the book where the author devotes himself almost exclusively to a historical account of the legend with only incidental moralization. In other contexts, Boccaccio describes his method in terms of Macrobius's four kinds of fable (*Genealogy* XIV.ix), and again according to Varro's three mythological aspects of theology which he found in St. Augustine (*De Civitate Dei* VI.v). He also offers an application of the four kinds of meaning to the *Aeneid* in which the three allegorical interpretations have nothing to do with Christian revelation;

the interpretation corresponding to anagogy, for example, finds Aeneas to be a type of the glory of Rome. Salutati shows almost the same eclecticism. In his *Hercules,* although he discusses the important similarities between the veiled modes of scripture and fable, he does not set up the customary categories of interpretation. But at least twice in his letters, in contexts which suggest a master-pupil relationship, he does invoke the familiar pattern of biblical exegesis.

Bersuire, who is interested neither in defending nor praising ancient poetry but in using it, makes only a brief and perfunctory comparison between scripture and pagan fable, and he says relatively little of his method of interpreting Ovid. He observes that scripture uses fable and fiction, and that the ancient poets wrote in a similar way when they represented historical and natural truth in their fantastic stories. He says that he will for the most part ignore the literal meaning, partly because it has been sufficiently treated by others, partly because it lies outside the intention of his work which is allegorical and moral exposition (Prologues to *Reductorium morale* and to *Ovidius moralizatus*).

So far I have dealt with aspects of fourteenth-century intellectual and literary history which are matters of ascertainable fact. I move now to the more troublesome area of opinion to consider ways in which this historical information may be of use to the modern reader of medieval poetry. If we regard the image —in itself and in configuration with other images in the context of the poem—as the essential mode of poetic expression, and the grasp of its manifold suggestive and evocative meanings as the responsibility of the reader, then it seems clear that awareness of the customary meanings of conventional images is an important part of the good reader's qualifications. While this critical generalization seems to me to be applicable to all good poetry, it applies in special ways to poetry written before the nineteenth century. It is certainly applicable to the best poetry of the Middle Ages, an art in which particulars are characteristically drawn from commonly shared and widely known traditions. Indeed, an obvious difference between medieval and modern literature is the medieval use of traditional figures and themes as opposed to modern preoccupation with the immediate, the novel, the idiosyncratic. I am aware of exceptions to this generalization among modern authors of major importance. The historical fact remains, however, that the Middle Ages valued the traditionally typical and exemplary in a way that is quite foreign to modern thought. Whether we approve of it or not, we cannot afford to neglect the medieval view of the meaning of experience, of man's nature and destiny, and the consequences of these views for the modes and meanings of medieval art.

But if it is granted that part of the meaning of the image is to be sought in the common poetic language of tradition, it is also true that the meaning of the image in its poetic context is unique, and that the act of criticism involves the discovery of this new and complex transformation of human experience. I would therefore claim for the information to be found in the mythographic tradition only a preliminary and general importance. The life of the image in tradition, whether in earlier poetic usage or in the writings of the commentators, is a matter of information, of learning, and therefore prior in time and ancillary in function to the discovery of its new and changed life in the poem. It is, however, indispensable, if we believe that the meanings and values mirrored in medieval images are not the same as ours, and that what the medieval poet intended, and what his contemporary readers received, ought to guide and enrich our own reading.

Such limited and preparatory usefulness is accompanied by obvious dangers. It may lead the learned reader, unburdened by the critic's awareness of the crucial importance of differences in the midst of similarities, to reduce the poem to unexceptionable generalizations. Or it may tempt the unwary to detailed oversimplification by way of mechanical identification. If we were to assume that the poem says what the commentaries say its images signify, we would reduce the poem to the status of another commentary, and the poem itself would escape us. For the poem's life, and the poet's achievement, reside in a new *mirabilis concinna mutatio* by which the traditional and conventional are transformed into a new and unique existence which alters and extends the tradition. What knowledge of traditional meanings gives us is a share in the point of departure with the medieval poet and his reader. The poem will then alter and modify, even trick and affront our conventional expectations. If we are alert to these possibilities, we may follow the process of change and escape the traps sets by the poet's ironies. If not, we will flatten out the poem to fit our simple preconceptions.

In spite of the dangers, awareness of traditional interpretations can save us from gross underestimation of the poem's possibilities (for example, the notion that figures taken from classical fable are merely decorative, or trite, because they may seem so to us), and from gross mistakes in understanding (for example, the notion that the Well of Narcissus is without serious moral implications for the lover who looks into it). Positively, such information can establish the general areas of meaning and value within which the poet may be expected to maneuver (for example, the commonplace that Aeneas's love for Dido represents a failure of intelligence and will, and a denial of his destiny).

It is perhaps unnecessary to say that I do not regard the critical use of mythological commentary merely as a means of solving cruxes, of filling in some of the gaps in received accounts of fourteenth-century poetry. I am proposing the use of appropriate historical knowledge to ask new questions about matters which, in my view, have not troubled the modern reader enough. On the other hand, I do not suppose that these new questions, and such answers as the mythological tradition may suggest and support, are the only questions to ask or the only answers to value.

I should like now to illustrate some of the critical uses to which familiarity with the fourteenth-century interpretations of classical fable may be put. The examples are from Chaucer, and they are chosen to illustrate different kinds of poetic situations. The first is from the *Friar's Tale,* a single allusion to the poetic tradition which suddenly illuminates the moral dimensions of a moment in the action, then is gradually seen to affect the action as a whole. The Friar's Summoner, you will recall, is on his way to extort a bribe from an old widow. He meets and joins a yeoman, and before long finds that he has made a fiend from hell the companion of his journey. In their conversation, the Summoner tries to learn what he can about devils and their methods, and he does, in fact, learn a good deal, especially about temptation.

Then the fiend-yeoman becomes impatient and remarks rather testily:

> But o thyng warne I thee, I wol nat jape,—
> Thou wolt algates wite how we been shape;
> Thou shalt hereafterward, my brother deere,
> Come there thee nedeth nat of me to leere.
> For thou shalt, by thyn owene experience,
> Konne in a chayer rede of this sentence
> Bet than Virgile, while he was on lyve,
> Or Dant also. Now lat us ryde blyve. (ll. 1513–20)

First and most obviously, this is a rather learned joke, and the immediate significance of the mention of Virgil and Dante would have been clear to readers of poetry in Chaucer's audience. Aeneas's descent into the underworld, in the sixth book of Virgil's epic, and the pilgrim-Dante's journey through the Inferno, were among the best known stories in ancient and medieval poetry. They were also, in the late fourteenth century, regarded as among the most profound, morally and theologically. Virgil and Dante were among the few men who, while still "on lyve," had experienced the poetic vision of the other world and had revealed its mysteries in poetry. Their readers could make the descent with them and, having learned the secrets of the devil's *privetee,* could amend their lives and so avoid that journey in actual experience. Superficially, the allusion comments on the irony of the Summoner's insistent curiosity—he will learn about hell soon enough at first hand, and he will then know more about it than the poets knew.

So much is obvious. But Chaucer is here invoking one of the

major moral commonplaces of the poetic tradition of classical fable—the topos of the *descensus ad inferos*—by recalling two of the most famous figures in poetry who had made the descent and profited by its figurative meaning. I give a brief account of it taken from the version in Salutati's *De laboribus Herculis* (IV.iv). There are four kinds of descent into hell a man can make in this life: the natural, the magic, the vicious, and the virtuous. The natural is the descent of the rational soul into the body in this world, a notion derived from Plato's *Timaeus* through the commentary of Chalcidius, and incorporated in Macrobius's commentary on Cicero's *Somnium Scipionis*. Through his encounter with the grossness of the world and the weakness of the flesh, the soul longs for the freedom of spiritual existence which he still remembers. The magic descent is made through necromancy, through the invocation of malignant spirits, rather like the situation in Chaucer's fiction. This descent, Salutati says, is rather an evocation of evil from hell to earth than a descent there. The third kind of descent, the descent of vice, is made by the man who scorns spiritual things and gives himself to viciousness. The fourth, or moral descent, is the imaginary journey into the underworld to contemplate the consequences of vice in order to ascend again to the practice of virtue. Some variation of this mode of interpretation was applied to the fables of Orpheus, Theseus, Amphiarius, Hercules, and Aeneas. And it was used by Dante's commentators to explain the pilgrim's journey through hell as the necessary condition of his ascent to Paradise.

These ideas would have been familiar to Chaucer's educated readers and would inevitably have influenced their response to

Chaucer's comic narrative. The Summoner is a knave and a fool whose lecherousness is exceeded only by his avarice. He has perverted his office and is as vicious socially as he is personally. In his encounter with the other summoner from hell, he learns what all men need to know, but out of mere curiosity, and so cannot profit by what he learns. His journey is a *descensus vitiousus* which ends in an actual descent from which there is no return.

I realize that all this is rather solemn commentary for a fabliau and I do not offer it as an account of the poem. I do, however, think that it is relevant to the commonly held moral viewpoint against which the ludicrous can be measured and appreciated. Chaucer's fiction is a kind of magic dream from which the narrator, in his own moral application of his fable, bids his audience *"awake."* I doubt that contempt for the contemptible friar who tells the story, and all the delightful ironies of the story itself, would have left the medieval reader entirely untouched by the mystery and terror of damnation which is the fable's burden.

Chaucer's *Knight's Tale* provides a different, and much more elaborate, illustration of the uses of the poetic tradition. The setting of the action in place and time, the dominant figure, and much of the descriptive detail are taken from the pagan poets. A brief and limited examination of the almost limitless possibilities of the *Knight's Tale* will suffice for the general purposes of this paper. No poem of Chaucer's has yielded more impressive results to criticism during the past ten years, a situation which makes it possible to ask new questions about its conventional features within a context of wide agreement about the poem's formal design and central theme. Moreover, the excellence and diversity of current criticism of this poem will serve to emphasize the partial and ancillary, but nevertheless important, use to which traditional interpretation of its fabulous images may be put.

In articles of major importance published ten years ago, Charles Muscatine and William Frost independently arrived at similar conclusions about the poem's meaning as the result of very different kinds of critical analysis. Muscatine's study was based on formal aspects of the poem's design, Frost's on the manifold implications of its subject matter. Among other results of their combination of the resources of modern criticism is the emergence of Theseus as the poem's central figure, the exemplar of the noble life whose speeches and actions are normative for the conflict of the rival lovers which dominates the plot. Theseus represents and invokes the principles of individual and social order which constitute the basic moral issue of the poem. It is precisely on this point that I think further analysis of the images, and especially those which combine to specify the role of Theseus, may extend and deepen, perhaps in some ways correct, the interpretations mentioned above.

The bond between the *Knight's Tale* and the fables of the poets is found in the figure of Theseus. Palamon and Arcite, and their love for the young Amazon, Emelye, with all its pathetic and happy consequences, are the invention of Boccaccio. The heroic figure of Theseus against the background of Athens, Scithia, and Thebes, is derived primarily from Statius, and Statius built on traditions derived mainly from Ovid, Virgil and Lucan, but the fourteenth-century poets exercised the freedom poets always have to draw at will from the much larger picture of the hero presented by the ancient poets and their medieval interpreters. Chaucer and his contemporary reader were familiar with the image of Theseus not only in the long history of mythological commentary, but in the appearances of the hero and his exploits in other poetry of the fourteenth century, notably in Dante's *Commedia*. Some of their resources are ours, and by a laborious process of reconstruction we can recover some of the knowledge, and a share in the attitude toward it, which they brought to the making and reading of poetry.

Chaucer's *noble storie,* a tale of "best sentence and moost solaas," is placed in the poetic tradition at the outset. After the epigraph from Statius, the Knight begins "Whilom, as olde stories tellen us" and introduces one of the best known heroes of classical antiquity, Theseus, lord of Athens. Twice within the opening twenty-five lines Theseus is identified as the conqueror who "with his wisdom and his chivalrie" had subdued "al the regne of Femenye, / That whilom was ycleped Scithia, / And weddede the queene Ypolita, / And broghte hir hoom with him to his contree." Chaucer's reader, familiar with the mythological tradition, would have recognized at once the implications of this famous incident. He would have seen in the struggle between Athens and Scithia the conflict between the city of wisdom, of rationality, protected by Pallas, and the barbarous land of appetite in which nature's laws were spurned by the warrior women. In the person of Theseus he would have seen a great hero of history, *vir fortissimus et gloriosus,* a peer of Hercules. He would also have recognized Theseus as a figure of the rational soul and its virtues, of the virility of rational action opposing the effeminacy of sensual indulgence. His victory over the Amazons would suggest the virile intellect subduing the feminine passions. The marriage of the Athenian king to the Amazon queen would be recognized as a perfect transformation in fable of the conventional use of marriage, the *copula maritalis,* as an image of the natural perfection of the human person in whom appetite is governed by reason.

This traditional image of the hero is extended and enriched by the incidents and allusions which follow in Chaucer's narrative. The invocation of his *pitee* and *gentilesse* by the Argive queens at the Athenian temple of Clementia recalls the legendary war of the Seven against Thebes, the symbolic opposition of the two cities, of Theseus and Creon. For the poets and mythographers this too was a fabulous representation of the victory of order over discord, of rational virtue over the shameful vices exemplified by the descendants of Cadmus. It would also have brought to mind the terrible consequences of the rivalry and hatred between the brothers Eteocles and Polynices which brought about the Theban war and ultimately the restoration of order by Theseus—a figurative context from which the new fiction of Theban "brothers," changed by concupiscence from friends to mortal enemies, will draw extended meaning.

As the hero leads his troops toward Thebes, we are given another *pictura* which complements the moral issues thus far raised obliquely by the poem. Shining in his white banner is the red statue of Mars, emblematic of his courage in war, and alongside, his gold ensign bearing the figure of the Minotaur he slew in Crete. I share Professor Muscatine's high regard for the beauty of this passage, and agree that its function goes deeper than ornament. But I suggest that it is more than an expression of Theseus's preeminence in war and chivalry. For the image of the Minotaur would evoke the memory of the hero's personal conquest of the monstrous product of Pasiphae's lust—a fable with obvious moral significance in the Knight's story.

Here, then, is an amplified view of the poem's affinities with medieval conventionalism, a fuller account of the noble life which Theseus represents, a traditional contribution to the normative values against which the poem asks us to measure the behavior of the young lovers Palamon and Arcite. Within this extended moral context the reader must take a rather more serious view of the antics of the rival lovers in their pursuit of the young Amazon, Emelye. A passion which leads to broken friendship, treachery, madness, and bloodshed would seem at least youthful folly rather than chivalrous devotion; Theseus's speech on the behavior of the lovers is an adverse criticism of disorderly conduct, rather than "a mature appraisal . . . of courtly love."

But at this point the most obvious limitation of analysis based on traditional interpretation of classical fable becomes apparent. It does not account for the way the poet handles conventional meaning—in particular, it provides no certain key to the circumstances of the poem and the tone that these circumstances convey. Indeed, given the scholarly seriousness, and often the religious zeal, of the medieval commentator, we may be tempted to transfer the philosophical and moral seriousness of the commentaries to a comic poetic situation, with disastrous consequences to the poem. The danger is apparent in our interpretation of the figure of Theseus in the complex tonality of the *Knight's Tale*. There is no question about the high seriousness with which he is presented as conqueror of "al the regne of Femenye," or as minister of justice to the tyrant Creon. And in much of the story of the rival lovers he remains the ideal "rex pius et justus" of medieval tradition, directing and interpreting the action. Still, it is impossible not to notice the urbane humor with which Theseus comments on the antics of the lovers. This serves to mitigate the seriousness of their folly, to qualify the dreadful implications of the conventional details in the descriptions of the temples of Mars and Venus. But in the complex processes of reading, there are many qualifications. If the indiscriminate use of traditional meanings leads to abuse of the poem, so too does preoccupation with literal detail, or with formal design and its implications. What we find the poem to be depends on the kind of questions we ask of it. I suggest that to ask what the instructed medieval reader would have made of the medieval poet's use of the figures and fables of the pagan poets is to ask a question of the utmost preliminary importance to the modern reader. And I further suggest that some useful answers can be found in the *olde bokes* of the fourteenth-century mythological tradition to which this paper has been devoted.

CHAUCER AND DANTE

Howard Schless

AT THE CONCLUSION of his *Anatomy of Criticism,* Northrop Frye summarizes the aim of the book in words that I would like to adopt, *pari passu,* to indicate the spirit of this paper. "This book [says Frye] attacks no method of criticism, once that subject has been defined: what it attacks are the barriers between the methods. These barriers tend to make a critic confine himself to a single method of criticism, which is unnecessary, and they tend to make him establish his primary contacts, not with other critics, but with subjects outside of criticism." [1]

To determine with some exactness the relationship of Chaucer and Dante, it becomes necessary to enter almost every sphere of Chaucerian scholarship. And one finds very rapidly the absence of what I must call (for lack of a better name) a contextual approach to Chaucer; that is, historical context when dealing with such questions as when Chaucer might have learned Italian or when the *Divina Commedia* might have been available in England, and literary context when dealing with questions of ascriptions—ascriptions which are all too often linked together *in vacuo.*

Obviously the time when Chaucer would have learned Italian or been able to read Dante will govern to a very great degree the dating of many of his poems, but this question is often colored by the critical view of the scholar. Thus, Tatlock was adamant in his assertion that Chaucer did not know Italian before his *Italienischereisen* of 1372 and 1378. What must be recognized, however, is that Tatlock's view is strongly in favor of what Kittredge magnificently termed "the neat triplicity"[2] of Chaucer's work into French (courtly and limited), Italian (humanistic and broadening), and English (realistic and mature) periods. Also, the indefiniteness with which he treats the date[3] and his desire to push it as far forward as possible are, one suspects, the result of his early dating of the *Troilus* (an "immensely endowed but inexperienced work"[4]) and his consideration of the *Parlement of Foules* as a mature and relatively late composition.

Surprisingly enough, one finds the same difficulties arising with some of the dating proposed by J. L. Lowes, particularly in the case of the *Hous of Fame* for which he feels there are two dates of composition, one for the Aeneid section (up to about l. 495) and another for the remainder from the moment where "Dante's presence makes itself felt [and] the poem is vivid with life."[5] Lowes hypothesized a date of 1379, stressing principally the idea that it follows the 1378 journey to Italy. This, he feels, is "a supposition which the presence of passages from Dante (whom Chaucer would certainly read as soon as he became acquainted with Italian) bears out."[6] Whether or not Chaucer would have read Dante first is a matter of individual conjecture, but what is most surprising is Lowes's implicit statement that

Chaucer was not acquainted with Italian until after the 1378 journey, for this not only seems contrary to the generally accepted date of 1372 or earlier but is contradicted both by Lowes's later writings and by a number of items in the list of works which he assigns to the 1369–79 period.

Could a definite date be reasonably offered for Chaucer's learning of Italian, or even for the presence of a copy of the *Divina Commedia* in England, the task of investigating the Chaucer-Dante relationship would be aided immeasurably; but lacking such information, it is only within the historical context of the place of Italians in the English society, and of the cultural relations of England and Italy, that one should approach the biographical problems of the Chaucer-Dante relationship. It is on the resolution of this problem—"and noght the revers, saufly dar I deme" [7]—that one's critical evaluation of Chaucer's development depends.

If it is desirable to maintain what Frye calls the comprehensive (and I a contextual) approach when dealing with biographical aspects of the Chaucer-Dante relationship, it becomes absolutely necessary when considering questions of source. By far the greater number of ascriptions have been made by Lowes in two early articles,[8] both of which are based on that particular kind of association of ideas best known by Lowes's phrase, "linked atoms." By this method, the lines in a poem that are said to be based on Dante have been suggested not on the grounds of a direct indebtedness but through the medium of another poem or poems; that is, a source (generally Boccaccio but at times some spot in the *Commedia*) contains a word or phrase that is said to remind Chaucer of a more or less similar word or phrase (in Dante), and this is offered as a probable source for some proximate word or phrase in the given Chaucerian passage. The assumptions underlying such a procedure would appear to be threefold: first, it must be assumed that Chaucer composed these posited Dantesque lines from memory (that is, without consulting the text, for this would often demand a more precise parallel than Chaucer gives) and, secondly, that he was capable of almost total recall of Dante (though not necessarily of other authors or common knowledge, which would break the linkage); finally, it must be assumed that on the basis of a limited number of works (usually Chaucer, Boccaccio and Dante), treated *in vacuo,* one can reconstruct the creative process of the poet. On the basis of these assumptions, one can then proceed to connect similar words or phrases in Chaucer's known source with others in Dante and thus attempt to show the extent of the influence of the *Divina Commedia.*

In the following investigation of the method, I am going to avoid largely those ascriptions that come from passages of invocation in Chaucer. Some appear to me to be quite valid, others to be more or less questionable. But all are involved with the *topoi* and conventions of invocation and are based on a reasoning so complex that it would be cumbersome indeed to carry out so minute an analysis in a paper such as this. Rather, I should like to examine some of the limitations of the method when it becomes too self-contained and fails to regard the period comprehensively.

We can begin where Lowes begins, with the list (as he gives it) of sixteen martyrs to love depicted on the walls of the temple in the *Parlement of Foules.* The acknowledged source is Book VII of Boccaccio's *Teseida,* but Lowes suggests the influence of the list of lovers in Canto V of the *Inferno.* Chaucer writes:

> Semyramis, Candace, and Hercules
> Biblis, Dido, Thisbe, and Piramus
> Tristram, Isaude, Paris, and Achilles
> Eleyne, Cleopatre, and Troylus,
> Silla, and ek the moder of Romulus:
> Alle these were peynted on that other syde,
> And al here love, and in what plyt they dyde.
> (ll. 288–94)

This list has been used as a case in point to show how Chaucer "incessantly fuses two or more bits of his reading into a *tertium quid.*" [9] On the basis of Boccaccio and Dante alone, Lowes suggests that "what has happened is clear at a glance"—Chaucer read the stanza in the *Teseida,* the third line of which "is echoing Dante," and this recalls the canto of Dante to his memory.

> The result [says Lowes] is that [Chaucer] combines Boccaccio's and Dante's lists into one. Not only is every lover in the Teseida included (through one at least of each pair) *but every name in Dante's list as well.*[10]

The assumption that underlies this view is that Chaucer is capable of total recall, that is, given the suggested echoing of the Dantesque line, Chaucer would be capable of calling to mind the precise list of names in *Inferno* V as well as a specific line therein. It is not that one doubts that Chaucer read this passage

—there is later evidence to prove that he did—but rather one wonders whether the assumption of total recall does not make the creative process more limited and mechanical than it would actually seem to be.

A comparison of Chaucer's text with his primary source, Boccaccio's *Teseida,* will perhaps prove illuminating in the present situation. On closer examination of the passage in the *Parlement of Foules,* we find that there are not sixteen, but eighteen, names, since Chaucer begins his list three lines before the point where Lowes begins:

> . . . of which [maydenes] I touche shal
> A fewe, as of Calyxte and Athalante,
> And many a mayde of which the name I wante.
>
> (ll. 285–87)

Now these two names, as well as the setting for Chaucer's passage, are in the stanza from Boccaccio preceding the one given by Lowes. And, these two are not "in Dante's list as well."

The two stanzas from the *Teseida* describing the paintings that Palemone's personified prayer sees in the temple of Venus, supply seven of the eighteen lovers mentioned by Chaucer. Of the remaining eleven, six *are* unique to Dante's list and these are: Dido, Tristram, Paris, Helen, Achilles, and Cleopatra; but these are the most famous lovers of medieval literature and Chaucer (who had used most of them in earlier works already) would scarcely have needed any source other than common knowledge to "recall" them. There is, then, not one unusual name in Chaucer (for example, Candace, Rhea Silva, Silla, or Troilus) outside of Boccaccio's list that is used by Dante and that would serve as a positive identification of source. Most astonishing of all, however, is the absence—supposing Chaucer were recalling the *Divina Commedia*—of Dante's greatest example of lovers, the main subjects of this canto, Paolo and Francesca da Rimini. Eminently suited as they are to the context, these two memorable lovers are conspicuous by their absence from Chaucer's verses.

Boccaccio may have started Chaucer thinking, but his thought would seem to have ranged wider than a simple *primus* and *secundus* leading to a *tertium quid*. Chaucer, who had already given a fair array of lovers in the *Book of the Duchess* (Paris and Helen, Dido and Aeneas, Echo and Narcissus, Sampson and Delilah, Phylis and Demophon, among others) and in the *Hous of Fame* (Dido and Aeneas, Breseyda and Achilles, Paris and Oenone, Jason and Hypsipyle, Jason and Medea, Hercules and Dyanira, Theseus and "Adriane," for example), was no novice dependent on sources for such famous names as the half-dozen that are found to be (upon comparison with Boccaccio's list) in *Inferno* v. If a source is necessary, the medieval versions of Ovid could have supplied seventeen of the eighteen names; and at least fourteen are found—many with their "fable"—in the *Ovide moralisé*.

As a matter of fact, Professor Lowes's later remarks on the catalogue of names from the first book of the *Hous of Fame* seem perfectly appropriate in the present case.

> The account [he says] of Dido's suicide is followed by a *stock list* of faithless lovers, drawn in part, either directly or by way of Machaut, from the *Ovide Moralisé*.[11]

The *Parlement of Foules* passage can be viewed in much the same way for, though we might not be able to point to one specific source, it is more likely that Chaucer's "stock list" developed from Boccaccio's stanza on the basis of common knowledge and reading in the standard classical authors.

If the "linked atoms" methodology faces partial limitation when confronted with common knowledge in the world of books, it encounters even more radical limitations from the extra-literary world of affairs. We find an instance of this in the passage introducing Jason in the *Legend of Good Women.* Professor Lowes suggests, not implausibly, the possible reminiscence of Dante's description in *Inferno* XVIII, but he then goes on to assert that line 1383,

> Have at thee, Jasoun! now thyn horn is blowe,

"translates the fifth line of the *next* canto of the *Inferno":*

> Or convien che per voi sueni la tromba.[12]

Echoing Lowes's note from Scartazzini, F. N. Robinson states that:

> The figure of the horn possibly comes from *Inferno* XIX.5, where it refers to the public crying of the misdeeds of condemned criminals. But the phrase *Have at thee* suggests that Chaucer had in mind rather the hunter's horn, sounded to start the pursuit of the game.[13]

Exception must be taken to this interpretation. The context in Chaucer makes fairly evident the meaning of the phrase. Chaucer, condemning Jason's falseness, says:

> Yif that I live, thy name shal be shove
> In English, that thy sekte shall be knowe!
> Have at thee, Jason! now thyn horn is blowe!
> (ll. 1381–83)

In other words, Chaucer is going to do all that he can to make known or proclaim abroad Jason's "sekte"—a term which will be dealt with shortly. This declaration is, of course, in keeping with Chaucer's promise to the god to serve as the champion of Love, and, having proclaimed his purpose, he formally issues his legalistic challenge. *Have at thee,* according to the *OED,* "is almost equivalent to *en garde* and announces the speaker's intention to get at or attack." In short, this line would appear to mean simply: Prepare yourself for an attack, Jason, for you have now been exposed as a criminal. This interpretation is borne out by one of the definitions of *horn* which, in Chaucer's time could refer to "the wind instrument as used in legal processes, e.g. in the *Scotch* ceremony of proclaiming an outlaw, when three blasts were blown on a horn by the king's messenger," [14] thus giving the phrase "to put to (or be at) the horn" to be proclaimed an outlaw, be out of the protection of the law. The procedure, then, existed in Scotch and Italian law, but there is still the question of whether or not there was a specific *English* equivalent.

Outlawry was invoked against an absent party as the extreme punishment; for the criminal was not even entitled to the law given "to noble beasts of the chase." [15] *"Caput gerat lupinum"* [16] —with these grim words the courts decreed outlawry. The procedure by the fourteenth century had lost much of its original brutality and was in the form of a formal public proclamation made in four successive county courts exacting the absent criminal. However (to cite Reeves) he

> could not be prosecuted to outlawry in this way unless a person stood forth to make the suit, who could speak *de*

> *visu et auditu* that the party had fled . . . and then he was to state the crime, as if the party was present and the appeal was going to be heard. . . . Thus not only *suit,* but the *appeal* was actually to be made before the fugitive could be outlawed.[17]

Formal proclamations were made to the sounding of a trumpet, and it is very likely that this legal procedure, plus Chaucer's formal presentation of the suit against the absent Jason, lay behind these verses.

If it is not outlawry that is being declared against Jason, it may well be the next similar legal action, the formal hue and cry, taken against persons who absented themselves (as Jason had deserted Hypsipyle and Medea) after the fact.

> The process [says Reeves] was to raise *hutesim,* or hue and cry, and a *secta* or suit was made after them from town to town. . . . The [*secta* or] suit was [then] . . . to be proclaimed in the county; a method . . . adopted in mercy to the absent fugitive who . . . by the old law was considered an outlaw upon his flight merely, without being proclaimed with this formality in the county court.[18]

Let us keep in mind, for the moment, the importance of the *secta,* as well as the formality of the legal action. Indeed, Pollock and Maitland give the specific procedure to be followed:

> When a felony is committed the hue and cry should be raised. . . . The neighbors should turn out with bows, arrows, [and] knives that they are bound to keep[19] and, besides much shouting, there will be horn-blowing; the "hue" will be "horned" from vill to vill.[20]

And the Select English Charters supply the specific procedure:

et tunc *cornaverunt* hutes.[21]

With this detail of procedure, let us join the technical term *secta* and the formality of a legally proclaimed hue and cry. Chaucer's lines are

Yif that I live, thy name shall be shove
In English, that thy sekte shall be knowe!
Have at thee, Jason! now thyn horn is blowe!

The passage is perfectly clear if we interpret it in terms of the legal phraseology of the fourteenth century. Chaucer (perhaps as Love's advocate) is raising a formal hue and cry against Jason, who has committed a felony by deserting (and causing the death of) Hypsipyle and Medea. Chaucer vows that his "name shal be shove / In English," and that his "sekte" shall be made known everywhere. He then issues his legalistic challenge and declares Jason an outlaw, to be put to the horn, a phrase that applies to the procedure of both initial outlawry and hue and cry. Jason's desertion and absence are being made a heinous crime, and Chaucer is following accepted procedure of *English* law in bringing formal charges against him, albeit more *de auditu* than *de visu*. By either procedure, however, the custom of putting to the horn was evidently as common in England as in Italy or Scotland.

Dante, in *Inferno* XIX.5, is not speaking about Jason, but rather the simoniac popes. This is another subject than Jason, with other lines and characters intervening, and to suggest that Chaucer's "linked atoms" worked by physical juxtapositions[22] when there is not even common subject matter is to give still wider berth to the ignoring of literary and historical plausibility. Thus it would appear that Chaucer, while he may have seen the process of putting to the horn while abroad, did not (to paraphrase Kittredge) have to make a long and complex journey—either physical *or* literary—to discover what he might well have observed at any law court or public square of the realm.

An additional danger of the "linked atoms" method is the embarrassment of unwanted links. I shall mention only two instances briefly. In the one, Professor Lowes in a very early article stated unequivocally, concerning the lines from the *Legend of Good Women*

> for vertu is the mene,
> As Etik seith, in swich maner I mene (ll. 165–66)

that "the one thing that seems at present to be clear is the fact that Chaucer's 'Etik' is not Aristotle but Horace."[23] In thus flatly rejecting Skeat and Lounsbury, Lowes was basing himself on the adjectival appellations found in John of Salisbury's *Policraticus* where the term *ethicus* is used for almost half a dozen classical writers, but most often for Horace. There he found not the precise phrase, *virtus est medium,* but one that might have reminded Chaucer (had he known Horace by memory or by text) of another epistle where *virtus est medium* occurs. But five years later Lowes was faced with the undoubted source in Tractate IV of the *Convivio,* where Dante's canzone states that "Vertute . . . (secondochè l'Etica dice) . . . dimora in mezzo solomente."[24] Lowes fails to state that this is an explicit reference to Aristotle's *Nicomachean Ethics* and, strangely enough, does not refer the reader to the very extensive discussion of the *Ethics* by Dante at Tractate IV in which the principal topic is virtue as the mean, and in which, again and again, the phrase *secondochè l'Etica dice* occurs. When faced with this new link, Lowes can only add, rather ambiguously, that "there is a similar passage in John of Salisbury, and between the two honors seem easy."[25]

A second embarrassment arises when following the links would lead to an obviously untenable ascription. Thus, the description at l. 64 of the second book of *Troilus:*

> The swalowe Proigne, with a sorowful lay,
> When morwen com, gan make hir waymentynge,
> Whi she forshapen was. . . .

This is closely modeled on ll. 13–15 of *Purgatorio* IX:

> Ne l'ora che comincia i tristi lai
> La rondinella presso a la mattina
> Forse a memoria de' suo' primi guai.

In his unpublished Harvard doctoral dissertation, J. P. Bethel is forced to approach this as "an interesting illustration of the way in which Chaucer uses Dante in combination with classical material,"[26] rather than as a purely Dantean source. The reason is that, later, in *Purgatorio* XVII, Dante makes it quite clear that he is following the *Greek* version of the story which makes Proigne the nightingale and Philomela the swallow. Therefore, Bethel must admit that "Chaucer seems to have been unaware of Dante's usage" of Proigne as the nightingale. "Unaware" avoids having to take into account the possibility (which would cast some doubt on the "linked atoms" assumption of total recall) that, while Chaucer used the descriptive tercet from *Purgatorio* IX, he simply did not remember the closely allied reference from *Purgatorio* XVII.

The final aspect that I should like to consider is the possibility of misreading—an almost totally unconscious act when one is working within the closed system of *in vacuo* source studies. It may happen in either the Italian or the English. As an example of the former, Lowes states that "Chaucer's conception of the Furies is marked by the recurrence of the idea of '*sorwinge* evere in peyne,' '*compleyning* evere in peyne,' and '*languishing*'"[27] —and he cites *Inferno* IX.37–51, which reads in translation:

> And more [Virgil] said to me, but I have it not in memory: for my eye had drawn me wholly to the high tower [of Dis] with its glowing summit,
>
> Where all at once had risen up *three Hellish Furies, stained with blood;* who had the limbs and attitude of women,
>
> And were girt with greenest hydras; for hair, they had little serpents and cerastes, wherewith their *horrid temples* were bound.
>
> And [Virgil], knowing well the handmaids of the Queen of everlasting lamentation (*etterno pianto*), said to me: "Mark the *fierce* Erinyes!
>
> This is Megaera on the left hand; she, that weeps (*piange*) upon the right, is Alecto; Tisiphone is in the middle"; and therewith he was silent.
>
> *With her claws each was rending her breast;* they were *smiting themselves* with their palms, and crying

> (*gridavan*) so loudly that I pressed close to the Poet *for fear* (*per sospetto*).[28]

Dante's Furies, though they might in one sense be "in peyne," are most certainly not "sorwynge." Indeed, one must recall the context of the passage in the *Commedia* in order to appreciate what it is that the Furies are doing. Dante is still in the fifth circle, where the sin of anger, *rancor,* or *furor* is being punished, and, as always in the *Divina Commedia,* the occupants of a zone exemplify the vice or virtue of their location. The tercet following Lowes's citation shows that the Furies that inhabit the City of Dis are not only not "sorwynge" or "languishing," but that they can only be thought of as being "in peyne" in the broadest sense that all the other tormentors of the Inferno are "in peyne," namely that they have fallen from grace. If Dante's Furies were languishing under torture, there would be no reason for him to say, "i' mi strinsi al poeta *per sospetto."* The following tercet shows that the Furies are not being tortured or tormented; they are tearing at themselves violently in an ecstasy of anger:

> "Vengan Medusa, si'l farem di smalto,"
> Dicevan tutte riguardando in giuso:
> "Mal non *vengiammo* in Teseo l'assalto."

"'Let Medusa come, that we may change him [that is, the intruder, Dante] into stone,' they all said, looking downwards. 'Badly did we avenge the assault of Theseus.'"[29] The reference here is to the rescue of Theseus from the control of these *medieval* Furies by Hercules. If Alecto is weeping, then, it is not from grief or torment but from the frustrated anger of not being able to tear apart the new intruder.

Lowes's suggestion of ascription may be valid, but not on the grounds he offers. Seeking some unique quality common to both Chaucer and Dante in order to overcome the very strong classical basis of these lines, he stresses the "torture undergone by the Furies."

> It is very true [says Lowes] that Chaucer must have been familiar, also, with the phrases "tristis Erinyes",[30] "tristis Dirae",[31] "tristis Furiae",[32] but the epithet *tristis* is scarcely sufficient to account for his emphasis upon the torture undergone by the Furies themselves and *their lamentations under it.* The explanation lies in the fact that Chaucer's conception of the Furies is colored throughout by Dante's.[33]

But I would suggest not only that Dante's Furies are not undergoing torture but that they are quite conspicuously lacking in lamentation. Again, if a source is needed, Spencer's fine article on "Chaucer's Hell" notes that in Part III, metrum 12, Boethius describes the effect of Orpheus upon the inhabitants of hell.

> Chaucer [says Spencer], in translating Boethius, had himself written as follows: And the three goddesses, Furies, and vengeresses of felonyes, that tormenten and agasten the soules by anoy, woxen sorwful and sory, and wepen teres for pity.[34]

While this is certainly not being offered as a "source," it is a great deal closer than the directly contrary picture of the violent Furies given in the *Inferno.*

Finally, I should like to take an instance that is not so much an example of misreading as of the limitations that are put on interpretation when a poem is not studied as comprehensively as possible. It has been suggested that the whole of the moral ballade *Gentilesse* is based on Dante's third canzone in the *Convivio* and its subsequent explications. There can be no doubt that Chaucer was thoroughly familiar with the Fourth Tractate (indeed, with but one or two exceptions, it is the only Tractate from which there are undoubted borrowings); not only does the Loathly Lady in the *Wife of Bath's Tale* expand on the discussion at some length, but Dante's phrase "antica richezza" appears in the ballade itself. But the presence of *a* source on a subject so common as *gentilesse* should not lead us to exclude others in seeking to understand the poem. Dante, we are told, "is especially apparent in the general tone of the poem, particularly in the association, as in the *Wife of Bath's Tale,* of 'gentilesse' with Christ."[35] Now while this is not exclusively Dantean, there is the fundamental question of the extent of association of Christ and *gentilesse* in the ballade.

The discussion naturally centers on an interpretation of the opening line that speaks of "the firste stok." F. N. Robinson notes that the phrase is "surely to be taken (as by Scogan) as referring to Christ or God," and after citing the *Wife of Bath's Tale* (l. 1117) he continues: "Professor Brusendorff, on the evidence of a passage in Lydgate's *Thoroughfare of Woe,* applied the term to Adam and Eve."[36]

I agree with Robinson that the line does not refer to Adam and Eve, but if we assume that the reference is to Christ or God, some very peculiar readings evolve. First of all, the line which Robinson cites in the *Wife of Bath's Tale*—"Crist wole we clayme of him oure gentilesse"—does not refer to Christ either as "the firste stok" or as the "fader of gentilesse," but rather as the *giver* of such a virtue. So far as I have read, Christ is never referred to, even metaphorically, as "fader," a term which would, of course, have been close to a unitarian heresy. In addition, the phrase "firste stok" hardly seems applicable, even assuming that Chaucer was ambiguously referring to God and Christ at one and the same time; for God *created* man, he was not—nor is he yet—considered as being a part of the same "stock, origin or race" (to cite Robinson's gloss). Following this phrase, there come instructions to " folwe his trace," to sow virtue and flee vices; but one is to follow such a course not to attain the kingdom of heaven (which should logically come from an emulation of God or Christ) but because "unto vertu longeth dignitee / And noght the revers."

The second stanza again refers to "this firste stok," describing it in the past tense as having been:

> ful of rightwisnesse
> Trewe of his word, sobre, pitous, and free.

But now the description becomes distinctly awkward if it is Christ or God to whom Chaucer is referring. To say that God is "clene of his gost" is, to say the least, a pleonasm. And what would be the relevance of remarking that God or Christ "loved besinesse . . . in honestee," even though it is "ayeinst the vyce of slouthe"? And again, if *his* refers to Christ or God, what is meant by "but his heir love vertu, as did he / He is noght gentil, thogh he riche seme"? Now, unless Chaucer is referring to human lineage, the increasing confusion of the first two stanzas will become total when the third is reached. If Christ or God is referred to by the pronoun of "his heir" in line 12, then line 15—"*Vyce* may wel be heir to old richesse"—is totally meaningless.

It is evident, then, that the third stanza is speaking, first, of men; and secondly, of the fact ("as men may wel see") that "there may no man . . . bequethe his heire his vertuous noblesse" which is the property of ("appropred unto") no rank, status or condition ("degree"), but belongs to God. And it is God who chooses as heir to the *original* man of "vertuous noblesse" that successor who can serve Him (i.e., God). The confusion here is in the pronominal referents, but careful reading will show, I think, that "his heir," in both line 17 and line 20, refers to the same person, and that what is being passed on, through God's choice, is the first man's "vertuous noblesse", i.e., his *gentilesse.*

We are left with the problem of identifying the original man whose "vertuous noblesse" returns to God to be given again by him to someone worthy of it. A perfectly clear reading can be obtained if we take "the firste stok, fader of gentilesse" to refer not to Christ but rather to the first race of nobles, which is the "fader of gentilesse" in the same way that Chaucer is the father of English poetry. Such an interpretation is based on the traditional argument expressed in part in Andreas as follows:

> excellence of character alone . . . first made a distinction of nobility among men and led to the difference of class. Many . . . who trace their descent from these *same first nobles* . . . have degenerated. . . . The converse is likewise true.[37]

No difficulty arises if we recognize that Chaucer's "firste stok" refers to the tradition of "these same first nobles," that he is recalling an age when "this world was so stedfast and stable that mannes word was obligacioun." To prove *gentilesse,* then, a man must follow the ways of the "firste stok," of those who were of the first, *l'age d'or de la chevalerie*. This group was spiritually pure, honestly active, and opposed to sloth, "sobre, pitous, and free" and true to its—*his* in at least the first four lines of stanza two is modern *its*—true to its word. But the legitimate heir of such a noble can only inherit his material wealth, not his *gentilesse,* which, like any virtue, derives from God alone. Being subject to *human* laws, material wealth, no matter how long it has been in a family, may well come down to a person steeped in vice; but *God's* gift of *gentilesse* goes to him who is worthy of it—and here Chaucer gives a slight but brilliant twist to the refrain—*even though* that worthy person, that person who can serve God, wears a mitre, crown, or diadem—that is, is a bishop, king, or noble.

Considered thus, the poem, though it loses somewhat in religiosity, gains a unity and comprehension that are otherwise lacking. Admittedly, Chaucer is working much more with a whole body of traditional ideas. Such an interpretation means, of course, that Dante's influence is one among many and depends chiefly on the "antica richezza" theme—the one original element from Dante that Chaucer added to his otherwise conventional view of *gentilesse*.

And since it is only fitting to close a medieval paper with a *moralitas,* I should like to quote from Robinson's excellent review of Chiarini's book on the *Hous of Fame* as an imitation of the *Divina Commedia*.[38] Robinson seems to me to strike at the very heart of the problem when he writes:

> Chiarini, like Rambeau before him, constantly errs, because he sees the *Hous of Fame* from only one point of view. Both these scholars study it solely in its relation to the *Divine*

Comedy, and of course they find numerous points of contact. Dante embodied in his encyclopedic poem nearly all the philosophic doctrine and very much of the current learning of the Middle Ages, and the same ideas were bound to reappear in any poem of the period that dealt, whether seriously or humorously, with philosophic subjects. Chaucer had read Dante, and his deliberate quotations and unconscious reminiscences add much to the common stock of thought, which would in any case have been inevitable.[39]

NOTES

PATRISTIC EXEGESIS IN THE CRITICISM OF MEDIEVAL LITERATURE

E. Talbot Donaldson: THE OPPOSITION

[1] "Historical Criticism," in *English Institute Essays, 1950,* ed. by A. S. Downer (New York: Columbia University Press, 1951), p. 14.

[2] See the historical treatment of the matter by Robertson in the essay cited above and in "Some Medieval Literary Terminology, with Special Reference to Chrétien de Troyes," *Studies in Philology,* XLVIII (1951), 669–92; also that by Robertson and B. F. Huppé in the first chapter of *Piers Plowman and Scriptural Tradition* (Princeton: Princeton University Press, 1951). The evidence for a genuine claim by Dante that he was using fourfold allegory in the *Divine Comedy* seems weakened by such recent studies as R. H. Green's "Dante's 'Allegory of Poets' and the Mediaeval Theory of Poetic Fiction," *Comparative Literature,* IX (1957), 118–28.

[3] See Robertson, "Historical Criticism," p. 13, and Huppé and Robertson, p. 1.

[4] Wimsatt, "Two Meanings of Symbolism: A Grammatical Exercise," *Catholic Renascence,* VIII (1955), 19: I am indebted to Mr. Wimsatt's excellent paper for this reference to St. Thomas.

[5] *Quaestiones Quodlibetales,* VII, Quaestio VI, Art. XVI: Unde in nulla scientia, humana industria inventa, proprie loquendo, potest inveniri nisi litteralis sensus; sed solum in ista Scriptura, cujus Spiritus sanctus est auctor, homo vero instrumentum.

[6] Green ("Dante's 'Allegory of Poets,'" p. 121) speaks of St. Thomas's *effort* "to restrict the term *allegoria* to the mode of Sacred Scripture."

[7] Huppé and Robertson (p. 10) say that they in general exclude the commentaries of friars because the poet was anti-fraternal.

[8] R. P. Miller, in "Chaucer's Pardoner, the Scriptural Eunuch, and the Pardoner's Tale," *Speculum,* XXX (1955), 180–99, for instance, gives an excellent account of the patristic significance of the Pardoner's condition; but when he replaces Chaucer's spiritual (and physical) eunuch with the Fathers' scriptural eunuch, he seems to me to be depreciating the poem.

[9] B-Prologue, ll. 14–19, normalized spelling.

[10] Huppé and Robertson, p. 17.

[11] *Ibid.*

[12] *Ibid.*

[13] B-Prologue, ll. 20–22.

[14] See especially B-Text 7.1–5.

[15] *Quodlibetales,* VII, Quaestio VI, Art. XIV: nihil est quod occulte in aliquo loco sacrae Scripturae tradatur quod non alibi manifeste exponatur.

[16] Huppé and Robertson, p. 17.

[17] B-Prologue, ll. 23–24.

[18] Huppé and Robertson, p. 7.

[19] *Ibid.,* p. 17.

[20] *Ibid.,* p. 19.

[21] *Ibid.,* p. 22.

[22] B-Prologue, l. 34.

[23] B-Prologue, ll. 112–22; the emendations seem obvious, though, as the following quotation from Huppé and Robertson shows, Skeat's text reads *man* for *lif* and *hemself* for *hir comunes:* the reference of either pronoun—*hemself* or *hir*—is ambiguous.

[24] Huppé and Robertson, p. 27.

[25] T. P. Dunning, *Piers Plowman: An Interpretation of the A-Text* (Dublin: Talbot Press, 1937), pp. 39 ff; Greta Hort, *Piers Plowman*

and Contemporary Religious Thought (London: Society for Promoting Christian Knowledge, n.d.), pp. 69 ff.

[26] *Piers Plowman: The C-Text and Its Poet* (New Haven: Yale University Press, 1949), pp. 109–10.

[27] Huppé and Robertson, p. 27.

[28] Donaldson, *Piers Plowman: The C-Text,* p. 110.

[29] *Quodlibetales,* VII, Quaestio VI, Art. XIV: sed sensus spiritualis semper fundatur super litteralem, et procedit ex eo.

[30] Huppé and Robertson, p. 240.

[31] B-Text 16.176.

[32] B-Text 17.2.

[33] B-Text 16.1–89.

[34] "The *Moralite* of the Nun's Priest's Sermon," *Journal of English and Germanic Philology,* LII (1953), 498–508.

[35] *Ibid.,* p. 505.

[36] *Ibid.,* pp. 498 ff.

[37] *Ibid.,* pp. 501 ff.

[38] *Ibid.,* p. 506.

[39] *Ibid.,* pp. 506–7.

[40] *Ibid.,* p. 501.

[41] *Ibid.,* p. 507.

[42] *Ibid.,* p. 508.

[43] For a fuller expression of this interpretation, see my *Chaucer's Poetry: An Anthology for the Modern Reader* (New York: Ronald Press, 1958), pp. 940–44.

[44] "Historical Criticism," pp. 26–27.

[45] For the poem in its original form, see *Secular Lyrics of the XIVth and XVth Centuries,* ed. by R. H. Robbins (Oxford: Clarendon Press, 1947), pp. 12–13.

[46] "Historical Criticism," p. 27.

[47] *Ibid.,* p. 31.

R. E. Kaske: THE DEFENSE

[1] For the exegetical writers mentioned here and throughout, as well as for medieval exegetical writers generally, the basic reference work is Friedrich Stegmüller, *Repertorium Biblicum Medii Aevi* (Madrid, 1940–55), Vols. II–V. Biblical exegesis from its beginnings through the thirteenth century is surveyed by Beryl Smalley, *The Study of the Bible in the Middle Ages* (2d ed. rev.; Oxford, 1952); from the eighth through the fourteenth centuries, by Father C. Spicq, *Esquisse d'une histoire de l'exégèse latine au Moyen Âge* (Bibliothèque thomiste, Vol. XXVI; Paris, 1944). Since the completion of the present paper, two other general works of comparable importance have appeared: Father Robert E. McNally, *The Bible in the Early Middle Ages* (Woodstock Papers, No. 4; Westminster, Md., 1959); and, especially, Father H. de Lubac, *Exégèse médiévale: Les quatres sens de l'Ecriture* (Paris, 1959), 2 vols.

[2] In the order in which they are taken up in this paper, see "Langland's Walnut-Simile," *Journal of English and Germanic Philology,* LVIII (1959), 650–54; "The Speech of 'Book' in *Piers Plowman,*" *Anglia,* LXXVII (1959), 117–44; "*Gigas* the Giant in *Piers Plowman,*" *JEGP,* LVI (1957), 177–85; "The Summoner's Garleek, Oynons, and eek Lekes," *Modern Language Notes,* LXXIV (1959), 481–84; and "The *Canticum Canticorum* in the *Miller's Tale,*" to appear in *Medium Ævum.* Documentation found in these studies is not repeated in the present paper. My analyses of *Petrus, id est, Christus* and of the passage on Christ's leechcraft, both from *Piers Plowman,* have not yet been put into the form of separate studies; accordingly I note quotations used in them but postpone the usual piling-up of supporting references. For further pertinent examples not touched on in this paper see "Two Cruxes in *Pearl:* 596 and 609–10," *Traditio,* XV (1959), 418–28; and "Eve's 'Leaps' in the *Ancrene Riwle,*" to appear in *Medium Ævum.*

Translations throughout are my own; in rendering passages from the Vulgate Bible, I have followed the Douay version with occasional modifications.

3 *Der Dichter des Ackermann aus Böhmen und seine Zeit* (Vom Mittelalter zur Reformation, Band III, Heft 2; Berlin, 1926–32), pp. 311–12; cited by E. Talbot Donaldson, *Piers Plowman: The C-Text and Its Poet* (New Haven, 1949), p. 185.

4 *Doctoris ecstatici D. Dionysii Cartusiani Opera Omnia* (Montreuil, 1901), XII, 616.

5 Donaldson, *Piers Plowman: The C-Text,* p. 184.

6 *Ibid.*, pp. 191–92.

7 *Opera Omnia in universum Vetus, & Novum Testamentum* (Venice, 1732), Vol. VI, fol. 155[r].

8 Donaldson, *Piers Plowman: The C-Text,* p. 186.

9 *Opera Omnia,* Vol. VI, fol. 173[r].

10 Since the publication of my note "The Summoner's Garleek" (see note 2 above), Morton W. Bloomfield has generously referred me to copies of this work in seven manuscripts besides Bibl. nat. lat. 3332, and to MS notations dubiously ascribing it to Gilles de Rome, Thomas Waleys, and Marco da Urvieto. P. Glorieux, *Répertoire des maitres en théologie de Paris au XIIIe siècle* (Paris, 1933), II, 305, gives its date as 1281–91.

11 "Chaucer's Pardoner, the Scriptural Eunuch, and the *Pardoner's Tale,*" *Speculum,* XXX (1955), 180–99.

12 "The Doctrine of Charity in Mediaeval Literary Gardens," *Speculum,* XXVI (1951), 45.

13 "Absolom's Hair," *Medieval Studies,* XII (1950), 222–33.

14 It may seem that by concentrating entirely on the existence of exegetical imagery in these few passages from the work of two fourteenth-century writers I have overlooked the larger and more important questions implied by the general title of this discussion. The importance of the exegetical tradition for medieval literature is, I am convinced, enormous in scope and varied in kind; but until Old and Middle English scholars possess a sizable area of enlightened agreement about its existence and significance in just such specific instances as these, I do not see how the broader aspects of its importance can be profitably debated.

Charles Donahue: SUMMATION

[1] Erich Auerbach, *Mimesis* (Princeton, 1953), pp. 17–18.

[2] See Hermann Jordan, *Geschichte der altchristlichen Literatur* (Leipzig, 1911), p. 381.

[3] Within recent years, French theologians have given considerable attention to the theological and liturgical implications of the distinction between typology and allegory—allegory in the Greek sense, not in the sense in which Paul uses the word in Galatians 4.24. With particular reference to Origen, the distinction has been developed by Jean Daniélou, *Origène* (Paris, 1948), pp. 137–98, and still further by Henri de Lubac, *Histoire et Esprit* (Paris, 1950). The distinction is, in my opinion, of fundamental importance for the question of the effect of the exegetical tradition on the imagination of Christian poets.

[4] See J. E. Sandys, *A History of Classical Scholarship,* 3d ed. (Cambridge, 1921), I, 29, 149, 156, 344, 418–19. A recent and full account of Greek allegorical criticism is offered by Jean Pépin, *Mythe et Allégorie* (Paris, 1958), pp. 85–214.

[5] See D. Comparetti, *Virgilio nel Medio Evo,* ed. by G. Pasquali (Florence, [1937]), I, 128–46.

[6] Philo's debt to his hellenistic background has recently been insisted upon by Samuel Sandmel, *Philo's Place in Judaism* (Cincinnati, 1956). See particularly chapter 1 and the conclusions on p. 211. With citation of further literature, Sandmel discusses allegorical exegesis within the rabbinical tradition on p. 16. Such exegesis existed. It was, significantly, more daringly practiced in Alexandria than in Palestine. Always a recessive characteristic in the tradition, it encountered opposition and "fell into relative desuetude." See also Pépin, (*Mythe,* pp. 225–31), who is convinced that any tendencies to allegorical interpretation in the rabbinical tradition were a result of Greek influence.

[7] Both Father de Lubac and Father Daniélou argue with great learning against the charges of irresponsible allegorizing leveled

against Origen since ancient times. Both insist that the main line of Origen's exegesis is typological and firmly within the center of Christian tradition. Undeniably, however, there are in Origen "des éléments caducs, qui relèvent de la culture de son temps et qu'on appelle son 'allégorisme.'" (Daniélou, *Origène,* p. 175.)

[8] Pierre de Labriolle, *Histoire de la Littérature Latine Chrétienne* (Paris, 1947), I, 408.

[9] Philo himself, although his principal interest is the moral doctrine which he reads into the text, was still Hebraic enough not to question, as a general rule, the veracity of the text (De Lubac, *Histoire,* p. 19). His method differs, somewhat as Ambrose's does, from Greek allegory.

[10] *Confessions,* VI.iv, in *Patrologia latina,* ed. by J. P. Migne, XXXIV, 722, (hereafter cited as *PL*).

[11] See Gustave Bardy's addition to the third edition (1947) of De Labriolle, *Histoire,* II, 611–12.

[12] In, *PL,* XXXII, 640.

[13] Maurice Pontet, *L'Exégèse de S. Augustin Prédicateur* (Paris, [1944]), does not distinguish between typological and allegorical elements. At the center of Augustine's exegesis, however, Father Pontet (chap. 6) sees an insistence on the prefiguration of the New Testament in the Old. An exegesis so centered is, of course, primarily typological.

[14] *De Doct.* I.xxxv (39), xxxvi (40), in *PL,* XXXIV, 34.

[15] *De Doct.* II.xi (16), in *PL,* XXXIV, 42–43.

[16] *De Doct.* III.v (9), in *PL,* XXXIV, 69.

[17] *De Doct.* III.x (14), in *PL,* XXXIV, 71.

[18] *De Spiritu et Littera* IV, in *PL,* XLIV, 203.

[19] A common theme in Augustine's exegesis; cf. Pontet, *L'Exégèse,* pp. 370–74.

[20] In *PL,* XCIV, 698B. The translation is a slightly abridged version of the Latin text.

[21] Early English Text Society, 160 (London, 1922), pp. 76, 77.

[22] The classical collection of such passages is apparently that of

C. Spicq, *Esquisse d'une Histoire de l'Exégèse Latine au Moyen Âge* (Paris, 1944), p. 19.

[23] *Didascalicon* VI.iii, ed. by C. H. Buttimer (Washington, D.C., 1939), p. 116; also in *PL,* CLXXVI, 801.

[24] *De Scriptis* III, in *PL,* CLXXV, 12.

[25] *Didasc.* III.viii, ed. by Buttimer, p. 58; in *PL,* CLXXVI, 771–72.

[26] Dante is clearly of first importance for the pan-allegorical problem. He is not an exegete, however, and is besides far too complex to handle briefly. A paper of mine on the four senses in Dante's literary theory, read last year before the New York Medieval Club, is being expanded for publication.

[27] My handling of Thomas's theory of exegesis is much indebted to Spicq, *Esquisse,* pp. 273–88 and *passim.*

[28] Cassian, *Collationes* XIV.viii, in *PL,* XLIX, 962.

[29] *Commentary on Sentences,* Prol. art. v, ed, by Mandonnet (Paris, 1929), p. 18.

[30] *Summa Theol.,* Ia, I, art. x, ad 3.

[31] *Ibid.*

[32] *Quodlibetum* VII, art. xv, ad 5.

[33] *Ibid.,* art. xvi.

[34] *Moralia* xx.i, in *PL,* LXXVI, 135.

[35] VII.xii, ed. by Webb, II, 144. In *Romance Philology,* IV (1951), 350, Jean Misrahi called attention to the importance of this passage for the pan-allegorical problem. Cf. also Hugh of St. Victor, *De Script.* III, in *PL,* CLXXV, 12: "Habet enim sacrum eloquium proprietatem quamdam ab aliis scripturis differentem, quod in eo primum per verba quae recitantur de rebus quibusdam agitur, quae rursum res vice verborum ad significationem aliarum rerum proponuntur." One thinks, too, of Dante's distinction (*Convivio* II.i, ed. by Busnelli, I, 98) between the allegory of the poets and the allegory of the theologians. Perhaps it is possible to suggest tentatively that in *Quodl.* VII.xvi Thomas is not only giving a theologian's opinion but also stating and defending a common doctrine of the liberal arts faculties.

FOLKLORE, MYTH, AND RITUAL

Francis Lee Utley

[1] *Ernest Hemingway* (New York, Rinehart, 1952), p. 188.

[2] *Anatomy of Criticism* (Princeton, N.J., Princeton University Press, 1957), pp. 52, 162, 341–42.

[3] See the edition by Herbert Thurston and Donald Attwater (London, Burnes and Oates, 1956), II, 149.

[4] "Some Disputed Questions of Beowulf Criticism," *PMLA,* XXIV (1909), 220–73; see also E. E. Wardale, *Chapters on Old English Literature* (London, Kegan Paul, 1935), pp. 92–93.

[5] *Proceedings of the British Academy,* XXII (1936), 245–96; see the comments of Frederick Klaeber, *Beowulf and the Fight at Finnsburg,* 3d ed. (Boston, D. C. Heath, 1941), p. 447.

[6] "Approaches to *Beowulf,*" *Review of English Studies,* III (1952), 1–12.

[7] "Monsters Crouching and Critics Rampant: or the *Beowulf* Dragon Debated," *PMLA*, LXVIII (1953), 304–12.

[8] *Anatomy of Criticism,* p. 196. If Christopher and Jacquetta Hawkes are correct (*Prehistoric Britain* [Harmondsworth, Penguin Books, 1952], pp. 55, 77), the sun cult of the Beaker Folk of Avebury and Stonehenge replaced the earth goddess and phallic cults long before the "iron-heeled Protestants" came in.

[9] *Scrutiny,* XVI (1949), 274–300 (essentially the same as John Speirs, *Medieval English Poetry* [London, Faber and Faber, 1957], pp. 215–51). See also the correspondence by John Bayley, John G. Watson, and Q. D. Leavis, and Speirs's replies in *Scrutiny,* XVII (1950), 128–32, 253–55, and 18 (1951–52), 191–96, as well as the remarks in *Year's Work in English Studies,* 1949, pp. 79–80. Some of Speirs's flaws in method and fact I leave to the amusing paper presented at the Modern Language Association in 1957 by Rossell Hope Robbins, "Mr. Speirs and the Goblins."

[10] Speirs, *Medieval English Poetry,* pp. 220–21, 249–50.

[11] *A Study of Gawain and the Green Knight* (Cambridge, Mass., Harvard University Press, 1916), p. 199.

[12] "Is the Green Knight a Vegetation Myth?," *Modern Philology,* XXXVII (1935-36), 351–66.

[13] "Who Was the Green Knight?," *Speculum,* XIII (1938), 206–15.

[14] My article on "Some Sinful Biblical Tales from Sweden," scheduled to appear in 1960 in a homage volume for Archer Taylor, has some further remarks on this subject.

[15] "Why the Devil Wears Green," *Modern Language Notes,* LXIX (1954), 470–72. Heinrich Zimmer himself (*The King and the Corpse* [New York, Pantheon Books, 1956], p. 89) mentions hunter's green in the Gawain cycle without drawing the logical conclusions from it.

[16] *Medieval English Poetry,* pp. 236–37; *Scrutiny,* XVI (1949), 290.

[17] "The Significance of the Hunting Scenes in *Gawain and the Green Knight,*" *Journal of English and Germanic Philology,* XXVII (1928), 1–15, and (with some revision) Savage's *The Gawain-Poet* (Chapel Hill, University of North Carolina Press, 1956), pp. 30–48. Some support for my view of the fox may be found in Layamon's *Brut,* lines 20825 ff.

[18] Moorman, "Myth and Mediaeval Literature: *Sir Gawain and the Green Knight,*" *Mediaeval Studies,* XVIII (1956), 158–72. Speirs is likewise criticized by George L. Englehardt, "The Predicament of Gawain," *Modern Language Quarterly,* XVI (1955), 218–25. He accepts the pentangle as symbolic of the complete knight and man, but considers symbols as conscious artifacts of the artist.

[19] *The Great Mother* (London, Routledge and Kegan Paul, 1955), p. vii. Schema III for the four kinds of Mother is found facing page 82. The italics in the quotation are mine.

[20] I presented this view in December 1948 at the English Section I of the Modern Language Association, and was pleased to find what must be an independent confirmation in Speirs's *Chaucer the Maker* (London, Faber and Faber, 1951), pp. 135, 153–54. James Sledd's "The 'Clerk's Tale': The Monsters and the Critics," *Modern Philol-*

ogy, XLIX (1953), 73–82, recognizes both the marvelous and Christian implications of the poem, but says nothing of the Virgin. His "monsters" are not Grendel and the Dragon, but Walter and Griselda.

[21] *Harvard Theological Review,* XXXV (1942), 45–79.

[22] *Myth, Ritual and Kingship: Essays on the Theory and Practice of Kingship in the Ancient Near East and in Israel* (Oxford, Clarendon Press, 1958), pp. 273–74.

[23] *Myth and Ritual in the Ancient Near East: An Archaeological and Documentary Study* (London, Thames and Hudson, 1959), p. 11. For another qualified myth-ritual view see W. R. Halliday, "The Religion and Mythology of the Greeks, *The Cambridge Ancient History,* II (Cambridge, The University Press, 1940), pp. 607–8. I have been unable for this paper to give proper attention to the monumental treatment in *La Regalità Sacra: Contributi al tema dell' VIII Congresso Internazionale di Storia delle Religioni, Roma, Aprile 1955* (Leiden, E. J. Brill, 1959), but it is clear that it represents many widely varying points of view.

[24] *The Limits of Literary Criticism* (Oxford University Press, 1956; University of Durham Riddell Memorial Lectures 38), p. 62.

[25] "Symbolism in Medieval Literature," *Modern Philology,* LVI (1956), 73–81; see also his "Religion and the Teaching of Literature," *Religious Education,* November–December 1958, pp. 1–6. For a similar view of the unique in literature see Frye, *Anatomy of Criticism,* p. 361.

[26] See Arthur S. Peake, ed., *A Commentary on the Bible* (New York, Thomas Nelson and Sons, [1919]), p. 698, and Ezra P. Gould, *A Critical and Exegetical Commentary on the Gospel According to St. Mark* (New York, Charles Scribner's Sons, 1913), p. 276.

[27] John Lydenburg, "Nature Myth in Faulkner's 'The Bear,'" *American Literature,* XXIV (1952), 62–72; R. W. B. Lewis, "The Hero in the New World: William Faulkner's 'The Bear,'" *Kenyon Review,* XIII (1952), 641–60.

[28] For the tangle which awaits the future critic see Lucia Dickerson, "Portrait of the Artist as a Jung Man," *Kenyon Review,* XXI (1959),

58–83 (on Philip Newby's use of classical, alchemical, Celtic, and Jungian systems).

[29] See, for instance, Margaret Dean-Smith, "The Life-Cycle or Folk Play," *Folklore,* LXV (1958), 237–53.

[30] *Medieval English Literature,* pp. 339–40. See *Year's Work in English Studies,* 1951, pp. 85–86, for the original articles in *Scrutiny.* See also Arthur Brown, "Folklore Elements in the Medieval Drama," *Folklore,* LXIII (1952), 65–78, and for the broader, non-genetic use of the term "myth-play," Frye, *Anatomy of Criticism,* pp. 282–83.

[31] *Folklore,* LXVI (1955), 288–94, 413–15; LXVII (1956), 103–5, 106–9. The slight bawdry and dance at the end of *Robin Hood and the Friar* (John M. Manly, *Specimens of the Pre-Shakesperean Drama* [Boston, 1897], I, 285) seem scarcely enough evidence to erect a ritual on. Bawdry in any event survives ceremony.

[32] For the whole controversy see the sources cited above.

[33] "Theories and Fantasies Concerning Robin Hood," *Southern Folklore Quarterly,* XX (1956), 108–15. A separate treatment of the many possibilities of interpretation of the Robin Hood story is found in several articles by William E. Simeone: "The May Games and the Robin Hood Legend," *Journal of American Folklore,* LXIV (1951), 265–74; "Robin Hood and Some Other Outlaws," *ibid.,* LXXI (1958), 27–33; "The Mythical Robin Hood," *Western Folklore,* XVII (1958), 21–28; see also Jay Williams, "More about Robin Hood" and "Still More about Robin Hood," *Journal of American Folklore,* LXV (1952), 304–5, 418–20 (Williams defends the Raglan point of view).

[34] *Sewanee Review,* LXVII (1950), 305–16.

[35] *Paul Bunyan, Last of the Frontier Demigods* (Philadelphia, University of Pennsylvania Press, 1952).

[36] "The Study of Folk Literature: Its Scope and Use," *Journal of American Folklore,* LXXI (1958), 139–48.

[37] *Folklore,* LXIX (1958), 1–25. For this question of folklore in the romances one might note Wolfgang Mohr, "Parzival und die Ritter: Von einfacher Form zum Ritterepos," *Fabula,* I (1958), 201–13, and Joseph Szöfferffy, "Volkserzählung und Volksbuch," *ibid.,* pp. 15–18.

Mohr shows the similarity of that "symbolic" hero Percival to the *ingenus* of Hansel and Gretel and Kiddlekaddelkar, and Szöfferffy gives folklore analogues for *Valentine and Orson*. Of great importance to the problem is recent extensive work on oral formulae: see A. C. Baugh, "Improvisation in the Middle English Romance," *Proceedings of the American Philosophical Society*, CIII (1959), 418–54.

[38] See Stith Thompson, *The Folktale* (New York, Dryden Press), pp. 393–94.

[39] Stith Thompson, *Motif-Index of Folk-Literature: A Classification of Narrative Elements in Folktales, Ballads, Myths, Fables, Mediaeval Romances, Exempla, Fabliaux, Jest-Books and Local Legends,* revised and enlarged edition (Bloomington, Indiana University Press, 1955–58; the lengthy subtitle is given because of its relevance to the subject under discussion); Antti Aarne and Stith Thompson, *The Types of the Folk-Tale* (Helsinki, FF Communications 74, 1928.

[40] A similar problem arose with John W. Spargo's *Virgil the Necromancer* (Cambridge, Mass., Harvard University Press, 1934), which used the literary documents accurately enough. He was criticized by A. H. Krappe in *Speculum,* X (1935), 111–16, for failing to observe that many of these legends may have been the creation of Neopolitan *ciceroni*. But Krappe's argument in retrospect seems rather a priori.

[41] See Charles W. Kennedy, *The Earliest English Poetry* (Oxford University Press, 1943), p. 250.

[42] See my review of Marshall Stearns's *Robert Henryson* in *Modern Language Quarterly,* XII (1951), 495. The serious fable work of Bernard E. Perry can contribute a good deal to a study of the *Renart* tradition—see his "Fable," *Studium Generale,* XII (1959), 17–37.

[43] *Studien zur Germanische Sagengeschichte,* Vol. I (Munich, 1910).

[44] *Folk Tale, Fiction and Saga in the Homeric Epics* (Berkeley, University of California Press, 1946).

[45] *English Studies,* XXXII (1951), 56–63.

[46] Moore, *Secular Lyric* (Lexington, University of Kentucky Press, 1951), and Greene, *Early English Carols* (Oxford University Press, 1935). For modern survivals of this kind see Francis L. Utley, *The*

Crooked Rib (Columbus, Ohio State University Press, 1944), Nos. 133, 249a, 284, 352, and R. H. Bowers, "The Middle English *The Fox and the Goose,*" *Journal of English and Germanic Philology,* LI (1932), 393–94.

[47] *Medieval English Poetry,* p. 277. Kennedy, *Earliest English Poetry,* p. 280, doubts a similar identification in the *Andreas* by George P. Krapp. On a Welsh Summer-Winter reflex in *Gawain* see Roger S. Loomis, "More Celtic Elements in *Gawain and the Green Knight,*" *Journal of English and Germanic Philology,* XLII (1943), 172–74. See also Frye, *Anatomy of Criticism,* pp. 182–83, 187–88, and, for a treatment by a major folklorist, Waldemar Liungman, *Traditionswanderungen Rhein-Jenissei* and *Der Kampf zwischen Sommer und Winter* (Helsinki, FF Communications 129, 130, 131, 1941–45).

[48] "Historical Criticism," *English Institute Essays 1950* (New York: Columbia University Press, 1951), pp. 26–27.

[49] " 'The Maid of the Moor' in the *Red Book of Ossory,*" *Speculum,* XXVII (1952), 504–6. See also R. J. Schoeck, "The Maid of the Moor," *Times Literary Supplement,* 8 June 1951, p. 357.

[50] R. L. Chapman, "A Note on the Demon Queen Eleanor," *Modern Language Notes,* LXX (1955), 393–96.

[51] "Noah's Wife Again," *PMLA,* LVI (1941), 613–26.

[52] The paper is to be printed in the Proceedings of the Internationaler Kongress für Volkerzählungsforscher.

[53] *White Magic: An Introduction to the Folklore of Christian Legend* (Cambridge, Mass., Mediaeval Academy of America, 1948).

[54] Alexander Scheiber, "Two Legends on the Theme 'God requires the heart,' " *Fabula,* I (1958), 156–58.

[55] "The Prose *Salomon and Saturn* and the Tree Called Chy," *Mediaeval Studies,* XIX (1957), 55–78.

[56] *Morphology of the Folktale* (Philadelphia: American Folklore Society, 1958). See especially pp. 90–91, 96–97.

[57] *Anatomy of Criticism,* pp. 108–9, 188.

[58] *The Great Mother,* pp. 89–93.

[59] *Anatomy of Criticism,* p. 104.

CHAUCER AND DANTE

Howard Schless

[1] *Anatomy of Criticism* (Princeton, 1957), p. 341.

[2] G. L. Kittredge, *Chaucer and His Poetry* (9th ptg., Cambridge, Mass., 1951), p. 27.

[3] See, for example, J. P. Tatlock, *The Mind and Art of Chaucer* (Syracuse, 1950), p. 10.

[4] *Ibid.*, p. 51.

[5] J. L. Lowes, *Geoffrey Chaucer and the Development of His Genius* (Boston, 1934), p. 133.

[6] J. L. Lowes, "The Prologue to the Legend of Good Women Considered in its Chronological Relations," *Publications of the Modern Language Association,* XX (1905), 862.

[7] *Gentilesse,* l. 6. Unless otherwise noted, all quotations come from *The Works of Geoffrey Chaucer,* ed. by F. N. Robinson (2d ed., Boston, 1957).

[8] J. L. Lowes, "Chaucer and Dante's *Convivio,*" *Modern Philology,* XIII (1915), 19–33; and "Chaucer and Dante," *Modern Philology,* XIV (1917), 705–35.

[9] Lowes, "Chaucer and Dante," p. 706.

[10] *Ibid.,* p. 707. Lowes's italics.

[11] Lowes, *Geoffrey Chaucer,* p. 132. My italics.

[12] Lowes, "Chaucer and Dante," p. 714.

[13] *Works of Chaucer,* p. 849.

[14] The italics are mine.

[15] Sir Frederick Pollock and F. W. Maitland, *The History of English Law Before the Time of Edward I* (2 vols.; Cambridge, 1895), II, 578.

[16] *Ibid.,* p. 447. The note here reads: "Select Pleas of the Crown (Selden Society), p. 47. Y. B. 20–1 Edw. I, p. 237: 'crie Wolveseved.' "

[17] Reeves' *History of the English Law from the Time of the Romans to the End of the Reign of Elizabeth,* ed. by F. W. Finlason (5 vols.; Philadelphia, 1880), II, 279.

[18] *Ibid.,* Citations are given to Bracton, 124 and 125. This is an explanation of the procedure involved in the formal hue and cry. For the hue and cry in its extra-curial operation, see the following citation.

[19] See the Writ of 1252 in Select Charters. Pollock and Maitland's note.

[20] Pollock and Maitland, *History of English Law,* II, 576–77. The note here reads: "Select Pleas of the Crown, p. 69: 'et tunc cornaverunt hutes.' "

[21] See preceding footnote. The italics are mine.

[22] The suggestion would seem to be that Chaucer, writing of Jason, recalled Dante's reference to Jason in *Inferno* XVIII, which is less than sixty lines away from the reference to the simoniac popes in *Inferno* XIX, which Chaucer thereupon recalled.

[23] J. L. Lowes, "Chaucer's 'Etik,' " *Modern Language Notes,* XXV (1910), 89.

[24] *Il Convivio* IV, canzone iii, ll. 83–87. Dante's extensive explication of the passage is in IV.xvii. I have used *Il Convivio,* ridotto . . . da G. Busnelli and G. Vandelli (Florence, 1934).

[25] Lowes, "Chaucer and Dante's *Convivio,*" p. 33.

[26] Bethel, "The Influence of Dante on Chaucer's Thought and Expression," unpublished doctoral dissertation, Harvard, 1927, p. 194.

[27] Lowes, "Chaucer and Dante," p. 718.

[28] I have used the Carlyle-Wicksteed translation, which comes closest to the idea of "sorwynge" by (1) describing Prosperpine's kingdom of "etterno pianto" as "everlasting lamentation" (though this has nothing to do with the Furies directly); (2) translating "piange" as "weeps"; and (3) rendering "gridavan" as "crying." Reading this translation, one could perhaps get a sense of "sorwynge," "compleyning," or possibly even "languishing," but most other translators have recognized the far stronger language of the Italian original. Thus, "etterno pianto" continues to be translated as "eternal lamentation" (Norton), "sorrow that hath no cease" (Binyon), "woe" (Ciardi); but the action relating to the Furies themselves is greatly heightened: "piange" becoming "wails" (Norton), "clamors" (Binyon), "raves"

(Ciardi), and "gridavan" becoming "crying out" (Norton), "loud . . . moan" (Binyon), "mad wails broke from them" (Ciardi). The italics are mine.

[29] Dante's reference here is to the rescue of Theseus from the underworld (and, of course, from the control of these *medieval* Furies) by Hercules in *Aeneid* VI.392 ff.

[30] *Aen.* II.337; *Her.* VI.45; *De Raptu* I.225. Lowes's notes and italics.

[31] *Aen.* VIII.701. Lowes's note and italics.

[32] *De Raptu* II.219. Lowes's note and italics.

[33] Lowes, "Chaucer and Dante," pp. 718–19. The last italics are mine.

[34] Theodore Spencer, "Chaucer's Hell," *Speculum,* II (1927), 185.

[35] Bethel, "Influence of Dante," p. 320.

[36] *Works of Chaucer,* p. 862.

[37] Andreas Capellanus, *The Art of Courtly Love,* trans. by J. J. Parry (2d. ed.; New York, 1959), p. 35.

[38] Cino Chiarini, *Di una imitazione della Divina Commedia: La Casa della Fama di G. Chaucer* (Bari, 1902).

[39] F. N. Robinson, "Chaucer and Dante," *Journal of Comparative Literature,* I (1903), 293.